MERTON

THE TWENTIETH CENTURY

EDITED BY ADAM SPENCER

LONDON BOROUGH OF MERTON

SUTTON PUBLISHING

First published in the United Kingdom in 1999 by
Sutton Publishing Limited · Phoenix Mill
Thrupp · Stroud · Gloucestershire · GL5 2BU

British Library Cataloguing in Publication Data
A catalogue record for this book is available from the British Library.

ISBN 0-7509-2114-5

Title page photograph: Children of the Millennium Woodland, 1999 (see page 125).

Dedicated, with love, to:
Laura Dorothy Louise and James Stanley.
Adam Spencer, September 1999.

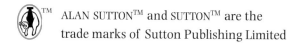 ALAN SUTTON™ and SUTTON™ are the
trade marks of Sutton Publishing Limited

Typeset in 11/14pt Photina.
Typesetting and origination by
Sutton Publishing Limited.
Printed in Great Britain by
The Bath Press, Bath.

Contents

Morden and Carshalton children's outing to Littlehampton, 1954. The *Merton and Morden News* had this to say about the trip: 'The streets of St Helier became a pilgrim's way last week. While the rest of the world was yawning and rubbing its eyes, 2,000 children were making their way through the side streets and pouring across Moreton Green to join a great pilgrimage of fun. . . . Thursday was The Day – the morning when St Helier was lined like a processional route, with parents waving handkerchiefs, as the 41 coaches pulled away. The procession cheered and waved back. Under a cold, damp, grey sky, a police motor cycle patrolman led the eleventh Morden and Carshalton Children's Outing on the first stage of its journey to the coast.'

Introduction

The opportunity to compile a photographic history of the London Borough of Merton in the twentieth century was an offer I could not refuse. After some thought, what I hoped to achieve became clear to me: here was a chance to make a contribution to the printed works on the area, working closely with colleagues in the Library and Heritage Services and with a publisher whom I had worked with on two other occasions. I hoped from the very beginning that, in collaboration, I could produce a work that would give an indication of the breadth and depth of the visual archive in Merton and at the same time provide an overview of the history of the district in the twentieth century. I was confident that the volume could be a success.

However, even after looking, quite clinically, at events and developments in the area over the last hundred years, having made notes and produced timelines of national and local events of import, we still had to begin selecting pictures. And we searched through and examined at least a few thousand images before we began to have an idea of what we could and could not achieve in terms of covering the events of Merton's history in the twentieth century. It quickly became apparent that trying to cover 100 years of history in about 220 photographs was not going to be an easy task. Inevitably many good photographs could not be included and I have to say that the process of selecting the images was both lengthier and more involved than I had imagined. Consequently, this book does not seek to provide a comprehensive account of the borough of Merton in the twentieth century. Rather it aims to give an evocative introduction to the history, and especially the visual heritage, of the four parishes that came to make up Merton. Although the bulk of the current selection is from the Library and Heritage Services collections, the compilation of the volume has also allowed me to access, in a limited way, the resources of other organisations. I have included a list of both individuals and groups who supplied images in the Acknowledgements on page 127.

As a consequence of the location of the majority of these images, a particular aim of this book is to introduce readers to the resources of the Local Studies Centre in Morden Library. I have attempted to illustrate the events and history of Merton, Mitcham, Morden and Wimbledon through the twentieth century with as diverse and visually appealing a selection of photographs as possible. Perhaps their publication in this book will encourage people to visit the Local Studies Centre for themselves. For every photograph included here, at least three or four have been discarded – an indication of the quality of the collection. I would like all readers to note that I would be very pleased to receive further information about any of the people, places or events portrayed in the photographs reproduced here.

The history and evolution of Merton in the twentieth century is not dissimilar to that of many other outer London boroughs. Administrative structures were set up early in the century which led to borough status for Wimbledon and Mitcham in 1905 and 1934 respectively. Although Morden and Merton began to agitate for such status prior to 1939, the Second World War intervened and they never gained borough status, but remained an urban district. At the start of the century the level of development in the parishes differed greatly; Wimbledon was by far the most developed and, with a population of 41,600 at the 1901 census, by far the largest of the townships. By contrast there were less than 1,000 people in Morden. Mitcham's population was around 15,000, Merton's 4,500. But then dramatic change occurred in Merton and Morden in just a few decades and they quickly lost their rural character to become outposts of suburbia. On the eve of the twenty-first century the population of Merton is estimated to be 180,000.

Overall, the period between the start of the new century and the First World War could be characterised as one of slow change, after which the dramatic effects of the conflict irretrievably altered the social structure of the country. The death of Queen Victoria in 1901 finally brought the long Victorian era to an end. She was succeeded by Edward VII, the coronation taking place in 1902. In 1911 coronation celebrations for George V were celebrated all over the country and locally and the pictures here reflect these events. As well as recording the changes in the administration of the area, which inspired a number of the photographs included here, some images also capture a glimpse of the rural atmosphere still evident in this period. Others show the development of shops, industry and public buildings, and portraits of some well-known local individuals.

From 1919 to 1938 the area underwent the greatest change in its history. Wimbledon was already populous, but during this period a great expansion took place in Morden. By 1938 the layout of the modern borough had largely been established, with transport networks set up and housing built. Similar developments changed Merton and Mitcham. Images in section two, which covers this period, portray sports teams, transport developments, new housing, Wimbledon's historical pageant in 1925, schools and industry, the visit of HRH Princess Mary to the Wilson Hospital in 1928 and examples of civic events such as lavish ceremonial openings of the new municipal buildings.

The long-expected Second World War began on 3 September 1939. Merton, as a collection of London suburbs, was just as much at risk of war damage as many other parts of the capital. The local population and administrative authorities were concerned with air-raid precautions, Civil Defence, and the possible need for evacuation. The war was to last for six years, ending finally with the surrender of Japan and the launch of the atomic age in August 1945. The 1939–1951 chapter is, of course, dominated by the conflict and the damage that was caused to this part of London by bombing raids. This section of the book includes pictures of society events just prior to the start of the war and postwar images illustrating schools, the Willow Lane fire, the decoration of Wimbledon children's library by students from the Wimbledon School of Art, the purchase of Morden Park and Cannizaro houses, and the continuing evolution of the transport network. It ends with the historic 1951 Festival of Britain.

The period 1952–1964 saw the dawn of the new Elizabethan age with the coronation of Elizabeth II in June 1953. There remained much postwar reconstruction to undertake and there was a marked civic, indeed national preoccupation with civil defence that would be necessary in the event of nuclear war. Although most food rationing ended in 1954 it was not until 1956 that shortages ended completely. Then, in 1965, under the provisions of the London Government Act 1963 the boroughs of Mitcham and Wimbledon were merged with the Urban District of Merton and Morden to form the London Borough of Merton.

Sections five and six include some lovely period photographs from the 1950s. We document the life of the Wimbledon Palais and the changes in use at the Majestic cinema in Mitcham. There is some evidence of the austerity of the postwar period as well as coverage of the joyful celebrations that accompanied the coronation of Elizabeth II. There are views of football and cricket teams, Mitcham Girl Guides, a charming portrait of Morden's postmen and a picture of The Goons, Mitcham's Lambretta club. The rising influence of the car is highlighted, as is the visit of Aneurin Bevan prior to the 1953 election. We close this part of the book with a view of Crown House, which became Merton Civic Centre in 1990.

Perhaps, in some ways, the establishment of the London Borough of Merton in 1964/5 was the defining moment of the century: it brought the previous administrations to an end and ushered in a new order. As was the case elsewhere in London, a number of dissenting voices were raised against the establishment of the new borough. However, the new Merton Council, originally operating from Merton Town Hall in Wimbledon, successfully undertook the task of working within the new political boundaries. Merton Town Hall opens the section of the book which covers 1965 to 1979, along with views of some of the elected members of the administrations that operated prior to borough status. The period witnessed the end of elm trees at Cricket Green in Mitcham and the closure of a large employer in Raynes Park, with the demolition of Carter's Tested Seeds. Images of Mitcham fair and the tennis championships at Wimbledon, the silver jubilee celebrations in 1977 and the events to mark the centenary of the 1871 Wimbledon and Putney Commons Act show the borough's people enjoying their leisure. Housing developments, the opening of Morden Leisure Centre and the decline of more traditional entertainment venues are also covered. Images of the changing face of the library service, schools, transport and shopping (with the opening of Tesco's in Mitcham) and pictures of the Buddhist Temple and Wimbledon Mosque depict the ever-evolving and multicultural nature of the borough.

The majority of the images used in the final section of the book, covering the years 1980 to 1999, reflect the emergence of the modern borough of Merton and give an indication of how it might evolve in the early twenty-first century. There are photographs of the changes in retail business, which reflect national trends – the opening of Savacentre at Colliers Wood, for instance, was an important local event. Similarly, the celebrations in Wimbledon after the upset caused by Wimbledon Football Club in the FA Cup in 1988 were important for the borough: the event perhaps refocused the public's mind to connect Wimbledon with a sport other than tennis! Developments in Wimbledon continue to provoke much interest and there are images in these pages of some of the new buildings constructed in the area over the last two decades. We have also included pictures representing the borough's heritage, including Wimbledon Windmill, the waterwheel at Merton Abbey Mills and Canons House.

American football, sailing and cycling are represented alongside Morris men, Merton's 1988 float for the Lord Mayor of London's Show, the fiftieth anniversary of Victory in Europe celebrations in Morden Hall Park, the visit of John Smith when he was leader of the Labour Party, the opening of Merton Heritage Centre and the unveiling of the refurbished Jubilee Clock. We also document further developments in Wimbledon, the great storm of 1987, a new transport infrastructure and have included a few pictures showing the 'future' for Merton.

I feel sure that I am not alone in lamenting the loss of some of the buildings and landscapes shown in this book. However, progress is dynamic and it is important to recognise that if destruction is unavoidable then full and accurate recording of what is to be lost must take place. It is increasingly incumbent upon us all to take part in the protection of our heritage. History is not only about yesterday, but also about tomorrow.

1900–1918

A 'Tank Bank' outside Wimbledon Town Hall, 14 March 1918. The First World War heralded the introduction of the tank as an important addition to British military hardware. The vehicle pictured here was christened *Egbert* and had recently distinguished itself at the Battle of Cambrai, November 1917. Its presence on the Broadway was intended to encourage local people to invest in war bonds. Just one week after this photograph was taken, the Germans broke through the British Front, north of the Somme. This offensive very nearly gave them victory over the Allies.

An idyllic view of rural Merton from the turn of the century. Merton Rush, pictured here in about 1910 was a cluster of old properties, situated at the junction of Watery Lane and Kingston Road. This view looks southward from Kingston Road. The shops of Merton Park Parade, dating from about 1907, can be glimpsed on the extreme left. At the end of the street are the timber cottages known as Dallett's Rents and next to them is Nash's off licence. Both properties were later demolished to make way for the construction of the maternity wing of the Nelson Hospital. On the right is a group of properties known as Cross Row with, on the extreme right, the Morden Hall Dairy Farm shop.

In 1902 Wimbledon joined the rest of the country in celebrating the coronation of Edward VII (see p. 12). Ox roasts were a popular addition to this type of festivity (see also p. 74). Here the ox is seen with Mr Lintott, the butcher who supplied it, outside his shop at 17 Hartfield Road. It had previously been paraded around the streets of Wimbledon.

Mitcham coronation day celebrations, 22 June 1911. The coronation of George V provided a last opportunity for the village to indulge in patriotic celebration before the outbreak of the First World War, after which nothing was ever to be the same. To mark the coronation there was a procession of decorated vehicles, including floats from local factories and representatives from Mitcham Fire Brigade. The old manual pump known as the 'Village Squirt' can be seen on the left of the picture. On this occasion it was driven by John Brown Jr, son of the local blacksmith. Travelling behind were the newer pumps including, on the right, *Caesar*, a second-hand Merryweather steam-engine, purchased by public subscription in 1884. It was named after Caesar Czarnikov of Mitcham Court, a wealthy sugar merchant and principal contributor to the engine purchase fund. Further celebrations included an Elizabethan pageant, commemorating Elizabeth I's visit to the Mitcham home of Julius Caesar Adelmare, Master of the Rolls, in 1598.

God save the King!

SOUVENIR

OF THE

Wimbledon Celebrations

IN COMMEMORATION OF THE

CORONATION OF

His Majesty King Edward VII.

Thursday, June 26th, 1902.

PRICE—TWOPENCE.

TRIM, TYP, WIMBLEDON.

HONI·SOIT·QUI·MAL·Y·PENSE

Frontispiece from a brochure celebrating the coronation of Edward VII, produced by Wimbledon Urban District Council in 1902. It is a bitter irony that, having waited sixty years to succeed his mother, Queen Victoria, the Prince of Wales was struck down by appendicitis two days before his coronation. He was finally crowned six weeks later, amid joyous celebration. In Wimbledon there were parades, fireworks, sports events and an ox-roast (see p. 11) on the common to mark the occasion. The council also hosted a Coronation dinner for the 'Aged Poor' at St Mark's church hall on 26 June.

Wimbledon Hill Road, *c.* 1905. At this time traffic in the area was still largely horse-drawn vehicles and delivery carts. However, the arrival of the motorcar was signalled by the warning notice 'Caution. This Hill is dangerous. Speed limit for motors reduced to 10 miles per hour half way down hill'. Notice the carved structure to the left of the road. This is a water fountain which commemorates Joseph Toynbee, an ear, nose and throat specialist, who died in 1866. Built in 1868, the fountain was a weapon against drunkenness, erected by public subscription at the suggestion of Canon Henry Haygarth, Vicar of Wimbledon and President of the local Anglican Temperance Society.

A rural scene, Cannon Hill Lane, 1911. This area marked the fringes of the Merton Park estate, owned and developed by John Innes (renowned for his horticultural and philanthropic work). The rich land was traditionally divided between a number of farms, including those owned by the Whatley family. It was purchased for new housing to meet public demand in the period following the First World War.

Visiting dignitaries. The Right Honourable David Lloyd George MP (seated in the car) visited Mitcham in December 1909, accompanied by his wife. He was probably there to support the local Liberal candidate in the forthcoming election. As Chancellor of the Exchequer, Lloyd George had recently released his controversial 'People's Budget' which increased taxes on high incomes and large estates. He is perhaps best remembered as Prime Minister in the coalition government that guided Britain through the bloodiest years of the First World War (see pp. 27–30).

Canon Wilson's jubilee, 1909. The long serving local clergyman, Revd Daniel Frederick Wilson was Vicar of Mitcham from 1859 to 1918. A tall, dignified yet somewhat aloof figure, he was ultimately an honorary canon of Southwark cathedral. He celebrated his fifty years of service in Mitcham in the 'flamboyantly Gothic' surroundings of Hall Place, home of the Worsfold family. Here he is pictured (seated, front row) accompanied by his wife (on the right, holding a bouquet) and various local dignitaries. These include Robert Masters Chart (back row, third from left, see also p. 40), John R Chart (back row, far right) and Alfred Mizen (seated, front) – all prominent businessmen and members of the parish council.

John R. Chart's seed shop at the corner of Fair Green and Common Side East, *c.* 1910. A description of the store by Tom Francis, a well-known local photographer, mentioned that the door of the shop had a tin bell and inside the atmosphere was distinctly 'mousey'. There were bins of oats and chaff and displays of millet, coloured packets of seeds and china eggs. Francis noted how the 'children experienced great joy in making [their] selection from the gaily coloured packets of garden seeds . . . spread before them by Mrs Chart'. Printing on paper bags of flour announced that John R. Chart was also a photographer.

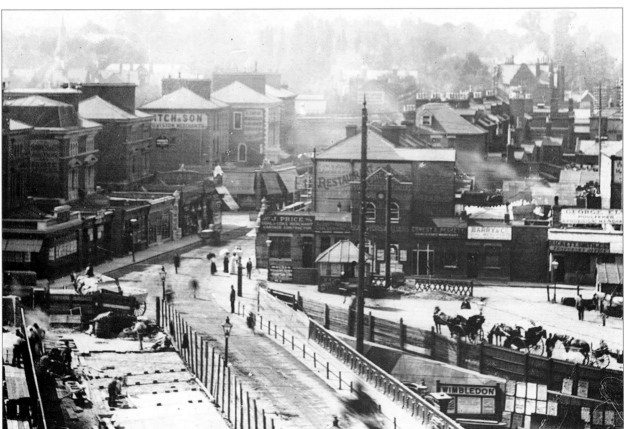

Wimbledon Railway Bridge, 1906. The original bridge, built in 1836, had to be widened in 1906 to take two sets of tram lines. Already, shop fronts had been added to the large neighbouring houses. The station entrance and cab stand can be seen to the right of the picture. This is now the location of the new taxi rank, constructed as part of the refurbishment scheme in 1997 (see p. 113).

Wimbledon Theatre, the Broadway, *c.* 1912. Opened on Boxing Day 1910, the theatre had one of the largest stages in the country. Lights ran off its own power supply and heat could be ducted into the auditorium from Turkish baths in the basement. Despite its many ups and downs, the theatre still flourishes. The casting of an 'angel', attached to its domed roof, has recently been restored and a £2.1 million National Lottery grant has funded a thorough refurbishment and expansion of the building.

The Masonic Hall, 78 Kingston Road. Opened in 1900, the hall was provided by John Innes. It was available for hire and many local functions were held here. Merton Lodge could not afford to buy the building after Innes's death in 1904, and had to vacate it. Merton and Morden Central Library was opened here in 1933, and it became Merton Public Hall in 1942.

Hill Road, Wimbledon, probably viewed from the bridge, *c.* 1912. Note the posters advertising property for sale, pasted on the walls outside Ogden, Sons & Olley's Estate Offices. Also, to the rear, note the preponderance of large painted wall adverts, for printers, drapers and a dental surgery.

Campaigning for office, Mitcham, 1904. Posters promoting candidates for the local parish council cover walls to the rear of Vestry Hall and the old Cricketers pub. Among the thirty-six candidates competing for sixteen seats were members of several prominent families, including: John Chart; the Mizen brothers (of market gardening fame, see p. 26) and Mr Drewett, who ran a funeral parlour at Fair Green.

A portrait of Sydney Gedge, *c.* 1900. Gedge lived at Mitcham Hall, a large white house situated off London Road, south of the Cricket Green. Tom Francis, from whose collection this image is taken, had little to say about the man other than that he 'was a great churchman, friend of the vicar, a public man, an out-and-out Tory'. In fact, Gedge, a Cambridge graduate, was a solicitor by profession and a licensed preacher in the sub-diocese. Churchwarden of Mitcham parish church, he was also active in the work of overseas missions and in 1886 he was elected MP for Stockport. After a break of three years, he returned to politics as the Conservative MP for Walsall in 1895. Locally, Sydney Gedge is perhaps best remembered for initiating work on the Mitcham Park development, an area of superior housing started in the late 1890s. Building work on the estate was interrupted by the First World War and did not resume until the mid-1920s. Sydney Gedge died in 1923, at the grand age of ninety-four.

A green giant, autumn 1906. Until after the Second World War prominent local households employed a small army of gardening staff, dedicated to producing fine blooms for the house and crops for the kitchen. This prize-winning marrow was grown by F. Batchelor, a gardener employed by a Dr Sedgwick. This huge vegetable was captured in all its glory on a postcard, dated 1906 and sent to Miss Sedgwick, 'Aunt Jane', presumably one of the good doctor's relatives.

Charter Day, Wimbledon, 26 July 1905. Described as an event 'never to be forgotten' by those who took part, 'this was the day when Wimbledon became a borough with its own Mayor.' The demands for a charter started in 1895, when the Local Board was replaced by the Urban District Council. Leading councillors argued that as Wimbledon had elected its own MP since 1885, it was entitled to the dignity of borough status. This was achieved during the glorious summer of 1905, when the new Mayor, Alderman Hamshaw, and the Town Clerk, Mr Butterworth, collected the charter document from Westminster. Crowds cheered as they returned in a procession of over forty carriages. A temporary balcony was erected at the Town Hall where Mr Butterworth read the charter to a gathering of dignitaries, seated behind a guard of honour from the Surrey Yeomanry. The Mayor, councillors and guests then attended a formal lunch at King's College School, while local residents were treated to a carnival procession, a military display and tournament on Wimbledon Common. As night fell, a celebratory bonfire and fireworks completed the entertainments. The charter was an official acknowledgement that Wimbledon had successfully transformed itself from the genteel village of the 1850s into much more than a London suburb. The charter was finally overridden in 1965 when Wimbledon became part of the new London Borough of Merton.

Wimbledon fire station, *c.* 1904. The brigade moved to these purpose-built premises, in Queens Road, in 1904. As the service became more professional, the status of the fire-fighters changed. From 1907 onwards, the engines housed here were manned by full-time paid firemen, rather than volunteers. The engines were drawn by a pair of grey horses specially trained to slip their heads into their collars as soon as the alarm bell went and the station's greyhound mascot would often accompany the brigade on call-outs. In 1913 horsepower was finally superseded by motorised transport.

Nelson Hospital, Kingston Road, soon after its opening in June 1912. Designed by F. Hatch, the hospital was the brainchild of a local doctor, Frank Deas, and took just eleven months to build, at a cost of £32,000. Though situated at Merton Rush, it served Wimbledon, Merton and the surrounding districts. The official opening ceremony took place on Friday 14 June 1912 and was performed by HRH Princess Louise, Duchess of Argyll. On the right is the entrance for private patients. A new wing was added in 1922 to commemorate local men who had fallen during the First World War.

The River Wandle, with mill wheel at Liberty's silk printing works, off Station Road, 12 April 1913. Earlier it had been known as 'Littler's Factory'. Edmund Littler moved to Merton from Waltham Abbey in about 1830. He established a business here as a printer of silks and wools, and by the beginning of the twentieth century the firm's largest customer was Arthur Lasenby Liberty, who decided to buy the works in 1904.

Shops on Merton High Street, c. 1910. This group of buildings still exists (much refurbished) between the bus garage and the Wandle. When this picture was taken, the proprietors of Wandle Marine Stores were selling an amazing variety of household goods and bric-à-brac. Notice the signs requesting horse hair (for stuffing chairs and mattresses) and white rags (possibly used for bandages, or rug-making). Also worth noting are the posters (far left) advertising the latest theatre and music-hall attractions, including *Harbour Lights*, a contemporary naval drama. As the 'Great Powers' amassed their armaments in the build up to the First World War, entertainment took on a more patriotic and in some cases nationalistic flavour.

Wright Brothers', milliners and drapers, Wimbledon Hill Road, c. 1905. Notice the fine array of hats and parasols displayed in the main window. Until the 1950s, everyone – from the poorest labourer to members of the gentry – wore a hat. Keeping one's head covered was traditionally a sign of respectability, while millinery styles revealed a person's status and financial standing.

Part of the manufacturing complex belonging to Morris & Co., Merton Abbey, 1913. William Morris was the leading figure in the nineteenth-century Arts and Crafts Movement. Multi-talented, he was renowned as a poet, political thinker and designer. In 1881 he acquired land and workshops on the River Wandle from Mr Welch, a local fabric printer. The site included timber workshops, water-meadows, gardens and a house on Merton High Street, in addition to good, clear water. Often with assistance from his friend, artist Edward Burne-Jones, Morris found the inspiration to create an amazing array of craft items, from printed fabrics and stained glass, to hand-knotted carpets and hand-woven tapestries. Much of this was sold through his shop at 449 Oxford Street. During his time in Merton, Morris was also deeply committed to the socialist cause and often spoke at local meetings of the Socialist League. After his death in 1896, the firm continued production under new management, with design input from Henry Dearle and Morris's younger daughter May. Rebadged as Morris & Co. Decorators Ltd (1905), then Morris & Co. Art Workers (1925), its fortunes took a downturn in 1932, with the death of Dearle. Declining interest in its products and the outbreak of the Second World War led to the ultimate demise of the company. It went into liquidation in 1940.

Wandle Park open-air baths, *c.* 1913. Opened on 30 August of that year, the baths were a popular source of exercise and entertainment until 1933. They were finally filled in and covered over in 1936. In accordance with contemporary views on propriety, this would appear to have been a ladies only session.

Road repairs at the top of the Broadway, *c.* 1910. The workmen have captured the attention of a number of inquisitive children, as has always happened on such occasions. The 'ganger' or works foreman is just visible in the right middle distance. The tram network reached Wimbledon in 1907 – note the sign (on the left) which identifies a request stop ('Electric cars stop here if required').

Old houses on the Causeway (the ancient name for the southern side of the Cricket Green, Mitcham), *c.* 1910. Tradition has it that the land was raised above the wetter part of the Cricket Green so that the residents of the Canons and the Cranmers could progress safely to the parish church. The building with the chimneys, on the middle right of the picture, is the old Victorian police station; it was replaced by the current premises in 1964. The pub sign in the middle refers to The Britannia, a Youngs brewery establishment just visible on the right. The nearby Kings Head is now better known as the Burn Bullock, named after a former landlord who was a famous Mitcham and Surrey cricketer.

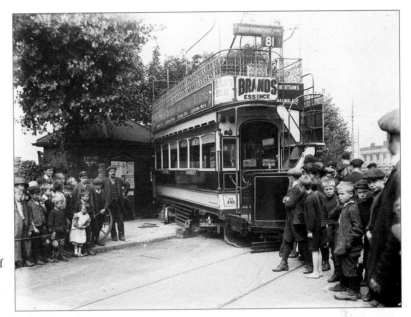

Off the rails! A tram derailed in Haydons Road, *c.* 1916. Any road accident seems to attract a crowd. Note the little boy with bare feet: poorer families could not always afford shoes for all their children. After an absence of many years trams will once again be a part of the transport infrastructure of Wimbledon with the opening of the Croydon Tramlink in 1999 (see p. 123).

Unveiling the fountain at Wandle Bank House, 1911. From 1791 to 1821, this was the home of James Perry, editor and proprietor of the *Morning Chronicle*, founded in 1770. Perry also owned the nearby Merton Corn Mill, rebuilt in about 1800 and recently used by Connolly's Leather Limited. A later resident of the house was Harry Pollard Ashby (1809–92), an artist and member of the Wimbledon Local Board. His daughter, Isabel, married Robert Bamfield Fenwick (1835–97) who helped to found All Saints' church. The two men were commemorated by a memorial fountain, seen here at its unveiling. Wandle Bank House was set in 10 acres of fine grounds. In 1907, the landowner, Mrs Ashby sold the estate to Wimbledon Corporation, with a view to establishing recreation grounds for Wimbledon and Merton. Wandle Bank Park was officially opened on Thursday 13 July 1907 by HRH Princess Louise, Duchess of Argyll. The Duke of Argyll and the Bishop of Kingston were also present. Wandle Bank House was finally demolished in 1962.

Putting spare time to good use, Mitcham Common, 30 May 1913. Increasingly alarmed by levels of unemployment, Mitcham Parish Council organised an emergency programme of public works. This included jobs such as levelling plots in the local burial ground and repairing footpaths on the north-eastern side of the common. Twelve men were employed on the latter project and paid a total of £24 2s 6d.

Mizen Brothers' nursery, 1913. In the 1860s Edward Mizen, a market gardener, acquired much of what had been the east field of Mitcham. Here, and at their other Mitcham nurseries, the Mizens raised flowers, vegetables and bedding plants for the London markets. Much of their produce was grown under glass. For virtually a century the business flourished in the hands of various family members, including Edward Mizen's three sons who were foremost among local horticultural growers. The Mizens' retail outlet in Mitcham was the Elm Nursery in London Road, which occupied the site of the medieval Pound Farm. Like many market gardeners, the Mizens turned their attention from flowers and pot plants to vegetable cultivation during the First World War. One suspects that several members of the nursery staff departed for the Front, although in some cases involvement in food production qualified men for exemption from military service.

In 1918 King George V and Queen Mary visited Merton to inspect local gardens and allotments. These were now an important part of the domestic war effort because U-boat attacks on the Allied fleet were causing serious food shortages. During the course of their visit, the royal couple spoke to wounded servicemen and the delighted Queen was presented with a piglet by staff from Wimbledon Park Piggery. Here the King and Queen are pictured inspecting a guard of honour outside Merton Church of England Schools, St Mary's Road, Merton Park. In the Boys' School log book, in red ink, Mr Johnson the Headmaster wrote: 'Their majesties the King and Queen amid the loyal manifestations of the children and other inhabitants of Merton visited our school gardens. The Chairman of the Urban Council, the Chairman of the Agricultural Committee and I were then honoured by being presented to their majesties the King and Queen, whom I escorted through the school garden. On leaving, the royal visitors expressed to me the interest they had experienced.'

The Holborn School, London Road, Mitcham, *c.* 1910, originally part of the vast Holborn Union Workhouse, which housed 1,000 paupers. The actual workhouse in Western Road was converted into a military hospital between 1916 and 1919. (It subsequently housed refugees from the Russian Revolution.) A stone plaque, once attached to the perimeter wall, and now in the possession of Merton Historical Society, commemorates patients and nursing staff who died during the the First World War. In later years the building was converted to industrial use. The last parts of it were demolished as part of redevelopment work during the 1980s.

Mitcham. - Holborn Schools.

Mitcham Town Guard, *c.* 1913. With the outbreak of the First World War, the ranks of the regular police force declined as officers were summoned for military service. The Town Guard was an auxiliary detachment made up of men from the Mitcham and Tooting area, including those who were unfit or too old for military service and members of reserved occupations. It was assimilated into the Special Constabulary in 1914. Notice the badges and armbands worn by the members of this force. During the conflict people were often hostile and suspicious of 'shirkers,' i.e. those who appeared to be dodging active service, and uniforms were in short supply, so special officers and servicemen on leave were issued with identity badges, to save them from embarrassment and physical assault.

Staff from Mitcham Red Cross Hospital. Founded by the Swiss humanitarian, Jean Henri Dunant, in 1863, the Red Cross was committed to upholding the Geneva Convention, providing medical aid and ensuring the welfare of victims of war. Many of the nurses, pictured here in 1915, appear to have adopted the new 'bobbed' hairstyle, which was more hygienic and easier to cover than traditional flowing tresses. A shorter skirt also made their uniform more practical.

Recuperating in the fresh air, patients and nursing staff at Morden Hall Military Hospital, *c.* 1918. When war broke out in 1914, the hall was converted for use as a military hospital at the request of its owner, Gilliat Edward Hatfeild. There was room for sixty-eight beds and patients benefited from the peaceful surroundings, regaining their strength in the freedom of Morden Hall Park. After the war, Morden Hall became an annexe of the London Hospital, providing convalescence for women and children. The wards finally closed in 1941, following the death of Mr Hatfeild.

Members of the 190th Brigade 'Wimbledon's Own', *c.* 1916. The final unit of volunteers recruited to form Kitchener's Army, the 190th was also the last of the 'Pals' battalions. These comprised friends, workmates and people from the same town, who agreed to serve their country on the understanding that they would remain together in one unit. Sadly this meant that many of them also died together on the battlefields of Ypres and the Somme.

Putting on a brave face, staff and patients at Morden Hall Military Hospital, *c.* 1918. After conversion of the hall for use as a military hospital (see p. 28) the patients were also allowed ready access to the house and gardens. This group may include troops from the British Colonies and Commonwealth Nations such as Australia. Injured servicemen wore distinctive blue felt jackets and red ties. This uniform was easily identifiable and was meant to deter the wearer from indulging in drunken behaviour or unauthorised absence during breaks from the hospital.

The canteen, YMCA hut, Wimbledon Common camp, *c.* 1917. During the First World War, many religious organisations vied for the honour of providing entertainment and moral guidance to the troops. In Wimbledon, the YMCA (Young Men's Christian Association) furnished clubrooms and erected a hut on the common. Here servicemen could enjoy a range of comforts including books and newspapers, billiards, card games and gramophone music. They could even pose for pictures taken by a resident photographer. The good ladies of the Church Army provided a selection of home-cooked food. Given the extent of wartime shortages, they appear to have amassed a huge selection of tinned and preserved food.

Postcard from Wimbledon Camp, First World War. Maintaining contact with loved ones was vitally important for those on active service. During the four-year conflict, millions of cards and letters passed through the military postal service. Humorous and patriotic illustrations were used to help maintain morale. They gave the impression that army life was carefree, but offered little insight into the true horrors of trench warfare.

1919–1938

Procession for Mitcham Charter Day celebrations, 1934. The charter conferred upon Mitcham the status of borough. This was seen as a tremendous honour, the source of much civic pride and public celebration. The festivities included a grand parade of carnival floats, with representatives from local schools and businesses depicting scenes from Mitcham's history. Here the procession is seen passing through Fair Green. Notice the Majestic cinema in the background; a popular entertainment venue, it had been open for just one year (see p. 76–7).

The development of modern Morden was closely linked with the arrival of the underground railway system. The local Northern Line station opened on 13 September 1926 and within a few years the peaceful farming community (see pp. 13 and 35) was swamped by new housing developments, including the London County Council's vast St Helier estate. This scene shows the underground station in about 1928. By this stage most of the adjoining retail units had been filled.

Morden Hall Road, showing the view south from Saddler's End and Morden Hall, *c.* 1931. Notice the motor bus in the middle distance and compare it with that on p. 49. The new flats at the end of St Helier Avenue are just visible in the background. The Morden section of the estate was complete by 1935.

Mitcham Athletics Club, *c.* 1920. The precise date of the club's foundation remains unclear. However, meetings are known to have been held at various local schools and hostelries since 1920. For the first three years of its existence, the club's president was Lieutenant-Colonel Bidder, perhaps better known for his archaeological excavation work in the locality. Initially membership was restricted to men, but in 1925 ladies' and youth sections were formed. The club enjoyed particular success in middle distance and cross-country events, winning medals at both local and national level.

The name of Wimbledon has become synonymous with tennis. In 1922 the All England Lawn Tennis and Croquet Club moved from Worple Road to its present site in Church Road. This 1926 photograph of J. Brugnon playing J.C. Masterman reflects the sports clothing of the period. Gentlemen taking part in the famous championships did not appear in shorts until 1930 and it was not until 1933 that such garments were considered suitable for play on Centre Court.

Wimbledon Historical Pageant, held in the grounds of Wimbledon Park House, June 1925. Large crowds gathered to watch the historical tableaux that formed the main attraction at the pageant. Prominent members of the community volunteered to portray characters from history, including Elizabeth I, played by Mrs Montgomery-Williams and Lord Burghley, represented by Mr R.C. Botwright. The event may have been inspired by the British Empire Exhibition, which took place at Wembley during 1924 and 1925. This event included historical drama in its varied programme.

'Last haytime, Morden, 1937'. This image, from a private album, is a fine example of the rural character of much of Merton and Morden well into the twentieth century. It is an evocation of a raw and picturesque landscape, which contrasted strongly with the extensive housing development that had already taken place. The remaining rural parts of Morden were to succumb to the developers soon as new housing schemes were implemented around Morden Park and in Lower Morden, where this picture appears to have been taken.

Mitcham Garden Village, *c.* 1930. Funded by Isaac H. Wilson, a local housing developer and benefactor, this estate was designed by Chart, Reading & Son as a peaceful residence for elderly people. Between 1928 and 1932 village-style housing was erected on part of Rowcrofts, a meadow belonging to the Cranmer family. The properties remain relatively unchanged today and the estate is still the quiet backwater conceived by its founder.

Wimbledon County School for Girls, *c.* 1939. The school was formally opened on 8 March 1924. This view of the domestic science room is just one of an impressive collection of photographs relating to the school. There are three albums in Local Studies Centre that chart the life and activities of the school from 1924 to 1947, although accompanying documentation suggests that the majority relate to the period 1939 to 1946. There are formal images of the staff, classes of girls and sports teams, as well as more unusual pictures of evacuation, postwar prize-giving ceremonies and the Drama Club. The school is now known as Wimbledon Chase Middle School.

Rutlish School, *c.* 1930. In 1687 William Rutlish, court embroiderer to Charles II, left £400 in his will to fund the apprenticeships of poor children in Merton. By 1894 this had grown to £6,000 and the money was used to build a science school under the guidance of John Innes. It opened in 1895 and offered a wide curriculum. In 1956 the school moved to Watery Lane, where it still exists. This building was demolished in 1970.

Mitcham gas works, part of the Wandsworth, Wimbledon & Epsom Gas Company, *c.* 1930. The Mitcham and Wimbledon gas companies were united in about 1908. Further amalgamations followed, resulting in the formation of the Wandsworth, Wimbledon & Epsom Gas Company.

William Harland & Sons, varnish manufacturers, *c.* 1920. The commercial manufacture of paint and varnish, potentially a highly polluting trade, became one of the main industries of Mitcham during the nineteenth century. Like many such companies, William Harland & Sons was based at Phipps Bridge. The firm was situated on land now occupied by the houses of Brangwyn Crescent (erected during the 1970s and 1980s). The successful manufacture of paint and varnish relied on a high degree of skill, experience and manual effort.

Opening day, Wilson Hospital, 2 November 1928. The hospital was named after its founder Isaac H. Wilson, a local builder and benefactor, who also financed the construction of Mitcham Garden Village (see p. 35). Chief guest at the official opening ceremony was HRH Princess Mary. She is pictured inspecting a Guard of Honour comprised of members of the St John Ambulance Brigade, under the command of Dr E. McKintyre.

Brownie Sixer, Jessie Cole, waits to present a bouquet of roses to HRH Princess Mary, at the opening of Wilson Hospital, Mitcham, 1928. The Brownies, the junior branch of Baden-Powell's Scout and Guide movement, were originally known as 'Rosebuds'. Their packs are divided into six principal groups, each with a different name and emblem. Every group, or 'Six', has a lead Brownie or 'Sixer'. The famous Brownie uniform has undergone a number of changes designed to increase its popularity and make it more practical to wear. This is one of the earlier versions including the formal tie and woollen hat.

An electric train approaching, Durnsford Road bridge, 1 mile from Wimbledon station, *c.* 1930. Steam-engines were still a common sight during this period. Electrification of the Kingston loop line was completed as early as 1916, but the main line to Woking was not converted until 1937.

A train approaching Mitcham Junction station, 1926. The tracks are pictured prior to electrification. The main line bears off to the right.

CHIEF CEREMONY OF
E DAY.—The Lord Lieut-
ant presents the Charter
oll to the Charter Mayor
r. R. M. Chart) and Mit-
:ham becomes a borough.

Mayor Robert Masters Chart receives the charter awarded to the newly formed Borough of Mitcham from the Lord Lieutenant of Surrey, 19 September 1934 (see also p. 31). The granting of borough status was an occasion for great civic pride and celebration. The 84-year-old Robert Masters Chart was the Charter Mayor. An architect by profession, he was also an alderman of Surrey County Council, former Mitcham Vestry Clerk and had been the holder of innumerable public offices, both paid and unpaid, for over fifty years. The Chart family had a remarkable record of service to Mitcham, beginning with the appointment of Robert's great grandfather, William, to the post of Vestry Clerk in 1761.

Coronation day party, Western Avenue, Mitcham, 1937. Similar festive scenes were witnessed up and down the country to celebrate the coronation of George VI, 'the reluctant King', and Queen Elizabeth. George VI came to the throne as a result of the abdication of his elder brother, Edward VIII.

The opening of the new Wimbledon Swimming Baths, Latimer Road, 21 June 1929. As at many swimming baths of the period, the pool itself could be boarded over during the winter months to allow the building to be used for exhibitions, concerts, and other events.

Streatham Road,
Mitcham, looking
south towards
Mitcham, 1930.
Caithness Road is off
to the left while
Ashbourne Road runs
off to the right.
Beatrice Ellen Bird sold
wines and spirits at
No. 221 Streatham
Road, while nearby
were Albert Kearle the
baker, Kleen &
Dunwell, dry cleaners,
and Henry E. Locker,
tobacconist.

Abbey Road at the junction with Nelson Grove Road, 1 January 1925. A number of similar photographs survive; they were taken by council surveyors to illustrate the poor condition of roads before resurfacing (perhaps in an attempt to justify the expense to the ratepayers). Note that New Year's Day was a normal working day in 1925.

Opposite, top: The eastern end of Worple Road, photographed from the Alexandra Public House, 2 October 1933. On the left is Ely's (see also p. 104), which had celebrated its golden jubilee seven years earlier with a banquet in the store. Beyond are the small shops now covered by Sainsbury's. On the right are the reconstructed shops on the pavement with Ely's store soon to be rebuilt with a new Odeon cinema alongside. Trolley bus wires hang over the road.

Opposite, bottom: Green Lane, *c.* 1935. This picture is from a collection compiled by the Merton and Morden Urban District Council Engineer's Department. It was the London County Council that preserved much of Green Lane, an ancient highway, between twin roads. This western section was restricted by development on the south side, leaving part of the old lane as a main carriageway (right). On the left are the Douglas Haig Memorial Homes for disabled ex-servicemen, opened in 1931, by the Prince of Wales.

Poplar Road School, infants' class, 1935. The southern part of Merton developed rapidly following the Underground extension of 1926 (see p. 32). Poplar Road School was opened in May 1932. Its rather spartan classroom, complete with long desks, provided accommodation for forty-two infants and their teacher.

Events in Mitcham seldom made the national headlines but an explosion in 1933 at the Church Road premises of W.J. Bush and Co. was an exception. The firm distilled oils and essences in the tradition of Potter & Moore, whose business they acquired in 1888. The devastating explosion caused extensive damage to the east side of Belgrave Road. One small boy was killed, twenty-three people were seriously injured and families living in cramped Victorian cottages in adjacent streets were made temporarily homeless.

The George Inn, Morden, *c.* 1926. Note the baker's cart belonging to Mr Adams of Central Road, whose premises were virtually opposite Morden post office. The inn is thought to have been established during the sixteenth century and, not surprisingly, its appearance has changed considerably over the years. The original hostelry may well have been known as the George and Dragon, while in its latest incarnation it has become a Harvester restaurant. There is also a motel on the site, catering for travellers on the busy Epsom Road.

Wimbledon High Street, 1930s. The Rose and Crown is visible on the left. This is one of a number of local pubs owned by Youngs brewery, based in nearby Wandsworth. The earliest photograph of this pub is thought to be date from 1875, when the Rose and Crown had its own stables and was the terminus for omnibuses to London.

Morden Hall Farm, with milk cart, 1920s. The farm occupied land west of Morden Road and north of London Road and Crown Lane. The trees in the background may be those of Morden Road. It was a mixed farm, but mainly dairy. Milk was supplied to local households twice daily, measured out straight from the churn, according to the customer's needs. Morden Hall Farm had once been part of the Garth family holdings, but when John Innes arrived in Merton in 1865 it became one of his early purchases. From 1866 the farm was managed for John Innes by members of a family called White. Oscar James White ran his Morden Hall Farm Dairy from here for more than thirty years until about 1920, with a number of shops in Merton, Wimbledon and even Tooting. In 1914 the farm occupied about 160 hectares (400 acres) and provided butter, cream, eggs and poultry, and Jersey and goats' milk as well as ordinary cows' milk. In 1926 the dairy was taken over by United Dairies. The pasture land was developed for housing, and the house in Morden Road was demolished in 1930, but the site in Kenley Road remained as a bottling depot until the 1980s.

Morden Cinema, 1933. The 1930s were the glory days of cinema. The local picture palace was considered to be a great asset, signifying the status and success of the district. Like many other towns, Morden was keen to have its own movie venue. Morden Cinema opened on Thursday 8 December 1932, amid great ceremony. Its opening feature, *Looking On the Bright Side* starring Gracie Fields, proved successful and local people continued to enjoy varied programmes combining action films with musicals, comedies, newsreels and cartoons. From Sunday 1 August 1937, the cinema became part of the giant Odeon chain. In addition to the big screen, there were variety shows, a 'Kids' Club' and fancy tearooms for the discerning customer. The rise of television led to dwindling audiences and the cinema closed to the public on Saturday 13 January 1973. For some years the premises were occupied by a DIY store, but then stood empty and decaying until the building was demolished in the early 1990s. This site is now occupied by an Iceland frozen food store (see p. 115).

Wimbledon Hill Road, *c.* 1922. Note the different forms of transport in evidence at this time, from horse-drawn delivery carts and 'pedal-power,' to the tram and motorbus. The bank buildings, pictured to the right, date from the late 1880s. The small shops situated opposite, with their distinctive first-floor windows, were built at around the same time. The local tram terminus once stood at the base of the hill, but it was relocated to the Town Hall in 1932.

London General Omnibus NS-type standing outside 5 Hartfield Crescent, Wimbledon. The destination board suggests it may have been hired, perhaps for a trip to a horticultural show. The NS-type motor bus was introduced to service in 1923. Vehicles were produced with covered tops in 1925 and in 1928 were fitted with pneumatic tyres.

'Please Miss, is jewellery spelt 'jewellery' or 'jewelry'?'– the original caption for this photo of a Mitcham librarian working with a young pupil in 1937. Mitcham Library was built in 1933 on land donated by Joseph Owen, a local builder and one-time Chairman of the Urban District Council, who also helped with the cost of construction. The helpful member of staff is thought to be Miss C.R. Black.

Felling a cedar, a well-known Mitcham landmark, outside 359 London Road. This 90ft tree, which once stood just beyond Cricket Green in the grounds of Mitcham Hall (see p. 18), was said to be 300 years old. It was felled on Monday 31 October 1938 to make way for a new garage.

1939–1951

Mitcham Rotary Club dinner at Mitcham baths, October 1939. Rotary is a worldwide organisation of business and professional men established by Paul Harris, a lawyer 'of humble parents', in Chicago in 1905. Archives of the Mitcham Rotary Club show that a little prior to the Second World War the club (of which the total membership was thirty-two in July 1937) organised international exchanges for children of Rotarians and vocational service for boys and girls leaving school, as well as the more usual ladies night, hospital carnival and charity cricket match.

Fancy dress, Mitcham, 17 February 1939. The *Mitcham News & Mercury* said 'The annual party and entertainment given by the Women's Section of the South Mitcham Residents Association took place on Saturday in the Parish Rooms, Lower Green. The children were in fancy dress and one tiny tot, with a representation of a fire-grate, bearing the inscription "We want Cole", took a prize for originality and topical allusion to the by-election to-morrow, in which Mr Cole is the Association's candidate.' It is difficult to know to what extent this electioneering helped County Councillor Cole, but he won the 'casual vacancy' for Mitcham Borough Council on a 34 per cent turn-out, roundly beating the only other candidate, Mr James Kennedy of Labour. On the left of the photograph is Alderman A.H. Bailey whose wife is standing on the far right.

The old school house, Morden, *c*. 1939. This building originally opened as a school in 1731, thanks to the philanthropy of Mrs Elizabeth Gardiner who had died in 1719 and left £300 to fund free schooling for the poor children of the parish. In 1872 a large hall was built on to it and in 1889 an infants' room was added to the hall.

A police sergeant in his back garden, Dorset Road, Merton Park, 1940. You can see the signs of air-raid protection – sandbags are placed around the base of the house as a buffer against blast damage and the windows are criss-crossed with tape to lessen the danger from shattering glass.

Wesleyan Methodist church, September 1940. A rear view of the damage to the Methodist church at the Green, Mitcham. The blast destroyed the church and blew the roof off the shops nearby. The Revd Blamey obviously kept his sense of humour in spite of the enormous damage inflicted on his church.

Recycling, *c.* 1943. The presence of a woman in the warehouse is a sign of the times. Because of the scale of the national emergency, women were increasingly being drawn into areas of work previously unfamiliar to them. In addition, in a bid to help the war effort, a wealth of items, for example paper and metal (the latter including garden railings, bicycles and old saucepans), were collected for the production of military hardware.

Model of Mitcham's corvette, HMS *Lavender*, 1941. Like many boroughs Mitcham wanted to give its name to a naval vessel and when £322,000 was raised during War Weapons Week, hopes were high. However, the level of demand persuaded the Navy to avoid naming ships after British towns as it was important to consider the blow to morale if a town's namesake was sunk. Given Mitcham's lengthy association with the production of lavender the name seemed an appropriate alternative. The purchase cost of an already commissioned ship was offset by the money raised locally.

'Fort Bailey' Air Raid Wardens' post 56, Mitcham Park, January 1940. Posts such as this were spread throughout the borough. They provided vital lines of communication during enemy action. Notice the piles of sandbags used to protect the building against blast damage, bullets and incendiary bombs.

Merton and Morden Urban District Council Auxiliary Fire Station No. 2, *c.* 1941. The fire station was based in the grounds of Joseph Hood School in Whatley Avenue and the trailer pumps shown in the foreground were among those used to tackle the huge number of fires that occurred during the Blitz. Thousands of incendiary bombs were dropped over Merton during the course of the Second World War. Approximately thirty-six were dropped inside a canister that burst above ground level, spreading its cargo over a wide area. A steel nosecap fitted with a detonator fired on impact, causing the bomb's thermite filling to burn at a temperature of up to 3,000°C, even without an external air supply. The thermite then melted a central magnesium core, discharging red-hot metal, which would continue to burn for up to 10 minutes. Sand had to be used to smother such bombs as a jet of water fed the flames and could even cause explosions.

Richmond Avenue, Merton,
20 September 1940. This scene was
the result not of enemy bombing but
the crash of a Junkers 88 that had
been hit by anti-aircraft fire. The
aircrew lost control over Wimbledon
and then crashed on numbers 2 and
4 Richmond Avenue. Although most
of the crew perished in the crash,
one aviator had baled out and landed
on a roof in Clapham.

Bomb damage on the Bushey Mead estate, Dupont Road, Merton, 1940. It received a number of hits during the Battle of Britain and again in 1943. In total some 16,000 houses in Merton were damaged and 275 families made homeless.

Bomb damage, Langdale Avenue and London Road, Mitcham. The tree in the centre of the picture originated from India and is thought to have been planted during the eighteenth century. Miraculously its roots were not even shaken by the German landmine which landed close and caused extensive damage to surrounding properties. During the later part of the war Merton suffered a number of raids involving V1 flying bombs (or doodlebugs) and their deadlier successors, the V2 rockets. At one point attacks became so frequent that Mitcham became known as Bomb Alley.

Bomb damage in Runnymede, Merton Abbey, 14 August 1940. A wartime news report commented that no one had been hurt when this bomb fell behind maisonettes. This picture shows the value of Anderson shelters, which appear almost unscathed in comparison with the burned-out cars and the rubble-strewn gardens.

The Friar Tuck British Restaurant, Mitcham, 1943. As the war progressed British Restaurants and Communal Feeding Centres were established to provide nutritious and reasonably priced food to augment wartime rations. Communal feeding also resulted in savings on food and domestic fuel, which were both in short supply. The Ministry of Food encouraged the decoration of British Restaurants with patriotic murals, usually depicting scenes synonymous with British life. (Here the decoration promotes the Dig for Victory campaign.) In some cases art students were commissioned to do the work. For instance, at the British Restaurant in Merton students from the Slade School of Art, working with artist John Piper, produced murals showing the historic buildings of Surrey including the ruins of Merton Abbey. Such scenes were meant to stir the national pride of the restaurant patrons, as well as enhancing the appearance of the building.

Braemar Avenue, Wimbledon, VJ Day, 1945. The war finally came to end on 14 August 1945 with the surrender of Japan after the use of the A-bombs on Hiroshima and Nagasaki. Of course the war in Europe had already ended in May 1945 shortly after the Russian army reached Berlin. Note the children's high-chairs, on the left; they could also be folded to form a small table. The railings had been taken from in front of the houses in 1941 to help the war effort.

All Saints' Junior School, Haydons Road, South Wimbledon, early 1940s. This is a lovely photograph of the swimming team with, at the back, the Headmaster Mr Baxter, who ran the school 1941 to1958. In the middle row, left of centre, is the Assistant Mistress, Mrs Loosen, who taught at the school from 1941 to 1964.

Sherwood Park Junior School, July 1950. Learning the times tables without the aid of a calculator. The dots on the blackboard help the children to calculate the answers more easily. Sherwood First School, as it is currently known, now also plays host to the Basic Skills Centre, a central government-funded initiative aimed at improving the skills and employability of local people.

Greengrocer's stall, Blunts Market, Hartfield Road, Wimbledon *c.* 1950. The stall seems to have an abundance of onions and rhubarb. Notice also how wartime rarities such as pineapples and bananas now appear to be more plentiful. The old-fashioned cash register is just visible in the centre of the stall.

Wimbledon Hill Road, 1950. Compare this image with those on pages 49, 73 and 84. They provide a 'journey' both up the Hill and across the years. Note the vehicles on the roads – the bicycles, the taxi, delivery van and split-screen Morris on the right – and the fact that there are fewer trees than in the earlier picture.

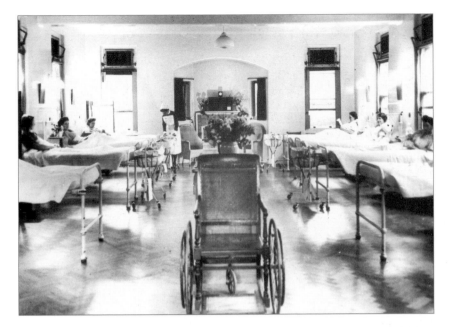

Nelson Hospital, maternity ward, 1944. This interior view of the hospital was apparently taken during war time. The building (see p. 20) was built in 1912 to replace the South Wimbledon, Merton and District Cottage Hospital, whose outgrown premises were in Merton Road. The maternity wing was added in 1931. Despite a number of scares about the prospect that the hospital might close, it is in fact still open. Before the advent of the National Health Service in 1948 most hospitals were financed by fees and public donations; as a well-funded establishment the Nelson earned a good reputation for its treatment and training regimes.

Road safety campaign, 8 January, 1949. A large number of children were present at the Odeon in Morden (see p. 48) for a presentation ceremony on the stage of the cinema. These young children collected their road safety certificates from a local policeman, Sergeant S.G. Osmond. Note the differences in clothing between the boys and the smartly turned out compere – the cinema Manager, Mr G. Harold.

W.J. Bush's Mitcham long service group, 1951. This picture was taken to commemorate the centenary of the Bush factory in 1951. All of these employees had worked for the company for a minimum of twenty-eight years, indeed the longest serving employee F.H. Priest (fourth from left, in the front row) had been with W.J. Bush for fifty-five years. In 1851 William John Bush, then aged twenty-two, laid the cornerstone for his fortunes in Bishopsgate, London. The company, which distilled oils and essences, flourished and Bush himself had a large family of seven sons and three daughters. Six of the sons later became associated with their father's business. W.J. Bush died in 1889. There is, perhaps unsurprisingly, no mention in the company history of the explosion at Mitcham in 1933 (see p. 46) but clearly the company survived this disaster to commemorate the anniversary of its centenary in 1951. In 1941, James Moreton Bush (who was third son of the founder) died, and the chairmanship passed out of the family to a long-serving company employee, Dr Isherwood. By happy coincidence 1951 was also the golden anniversary of Dr Isherwood's service with the company.

A view of the spectacular fire that began on 2 June 1947 at the Willow Lane tyre dump. The tyres had been collected during the war for recycling. The fire raged for days and a cloud of black smoke could be seen from miles away. Crews from several districts were called in to tackle this blaze. It is said that large numbers of frogs surfaced in the area surrounding the blaze, having been disturbed from their marshy habitat by the heat. The firefighters pictured here appear to be wearing wartime uniform – a tin helmet, a thick tunic, oilskin trousers and a belt with a pouch to carry an axe, lamp and other essentials.

Wimbledon School of Art students painting murals at Wimbledon children's library, 1947. After the Second World War the School of Art students undertook a number of ambitious projects, including works in St Mark's church and, seen here, a series of twenty-eight mural paintings in Wimbledon Public Library. This was, apparently, a deliberate policy of the school's principal Gerald Cooper. The paintings exhibit a definite 'Wimbledon' style. They are also reminiscent of work by Breughel and Stanley Spencer, whose daughter was a student at Wimbledon. The twelve largest murals depict the months of the year, while others show seasonal children's games. The fiftieth anniversary of the murals was celebrated when a small ceremony, attended by some of the original artists, was held in the library on Wednesday 18 June 1997.

Opening of the Grand Drive Co-op, August 1939. Here Jim Alexander has his photo taken serving Mrs Staseby on the opening day. The opening of the Royal Arsenal Co-operative store was a response to the residential development on both sides of the Morden end of Grand Drive.

Cannizaro House. From its construction in 1705 until 1841, this was known as the 'Warren House'. From 1841, it took its name from the owner from 1817 to 1841, the Sicilian Duke of Cannizaro. Perhaps because it sounded so exotic the name stuck even after the house had to be totally rebuilt on a different plan when a disastrous fire burnt all except the garden front to the ground in October 1900. The house was sold to Wimbledon Corporation in 1948 and the gardens opened as a public park. Its beautiful grounds now provide an oasis of peace on the edge of a very busy common (see p. 116).

Morden Park House, *c.* 1948. The mansion was built for John Ewart Esq, an eminent London distiller, in 1770, but he seems to have moved out around ten years later. For the next 150 years the house was home to a long list of distinguished residents including its final one, Lady Eva Cecilia Margaret Wemyss. In the 1930s it became a golf club-house, leased by the Merton Park (Wimbledon) Golf Club Limited. Between 1965 and 1985 it was the offices of the London Borough of Merton's Parks, Allotments and Cemeteries Department. It is now undergoing a long-anticipated refurbishment which will transform it into the new register office for Merton.

Pollards Hill branch library (above) and Morden Park branch library (below). Both Merton and Morden Urban District Council and Mitcham Borough Council realised that in the postwar period there was a desperate need for more libraries in their respective areas. Although not an obvious choice to house a new branch library, the Lower Morden Lane building (a purpose-built Civil Defence depot) was pressed into service. The Pollards Hill branch was replaced by a new building in 1970 (see p. 101).

Fashion parade, Morden, 22 October 1948. This show at Morden Urban District Council Offices took place in the era when clothes were still rationed in the aftermath of the Second World War. Here we see Miss Sheila Sim at the Co-op exhibition in Morden.

St Helier Woodcraft Folk, 15 May 1948. This photograph shows members of the Woodcraft Folk giving a sword dancing demonstration on Moreton Green. They were due to leave for their weekend camp shortly after the event. The Woodcraft Folk are still active in the borough, providing weekly meetings for children and young people and activities including games, drama, craftwork and camping.

Trams at Wimbledon, 19 November 1950. Here we see the Wimbledon terminus at the Town Hall. The photograph shows the only scissors cross-over on the postwar system and E-1 cars numbers 1838 and 1841 on routes 2 and 4. On the right is a trolley bus heading for Hampton Court on route 604. The trams were phased out in 1951 to be replaced by buses which also soon took over from the trolley buses on the route to Kingston. However, the advent of the Croydon Tramlink and the proposed application for an extension – the Merton Tramlink – will see the reappearance of trams in Wimbledon, although not on the streets in front of the Town Hall.

Merton Park crossing, c. 1950. This is the level crossing in Kingston Road (see also p. 100) built in 1855. Bridges had to be built where the line crosses Morden Road and London Road, Mitcham, because they were turnpike roads. Kingston Road was not a turnpike road. Apparently from the moment of the crossing's installation it became an almost continual source of complaint. It was the subject of much discussion in the 1920s and 1930s between Merton and Morden Urban District Council and the Southern Railway and in 1998/9, for instance, the flow of traffic was severely curtailed by the construction works necessary for the Tramlink installation. The level crossing has, however, survived. Just beyond the signal-box (constructed in 1913 and replaced by a system of automatic gates in 1984) are the remains of the White Hart. A victim of wartime bombing, it was not rebuilt until the 1950s. The new building survives, and is now an Irish theme pub called Bodhran Barney's.

MERTON & MORDEN

FESTIVAL of BRITAIN

(Sponsored by Merton and Morden Urban District Council)

SOUVENIR PROGRAMME
OF EVENTS

for the

CIVIC WEEK *to be held in* **MORDEN PARK**

from

SUNDAY, JUNE 17th, 1951

to

SATURDAY, JUNE 23rd, 1951

inclusive

Organised for the People of the District by their
Representatives in close co-operation with
Merton and Morden Urban District Council

**Price
Sixpence**

BOROUGH OF MITCHAM
ALDERMAN G. R. MADGWICK, J.P., MAYOR

MITCHAM PUBLIC LIBRARY.

FESTIVAL
WEEK

7-14 JULY 1951

*This programme admits one person to all events
with the exception of swimming galas and boxing*

PROGRAMME PRICE SIXPENCE

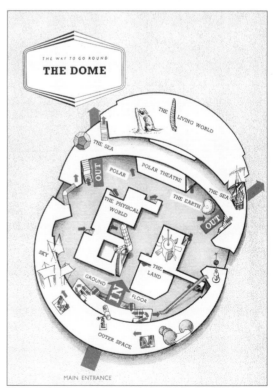

Festival of Britain brochures and the Dome of Discovery, 1951.
The Festival of Britain in 1951 was a countrywide celebration of
technological innovation and experience in the UK. These are
the front covers of the souvenir programmes of events published
by Merton and Morden Urban District Council and the Festival
Week brochure from the Borough of Mitcham for 7–14 July
1951. There is an additional and timely Wimbledon connection
for the 1951 festival. In 1939 Ralph Tubbs, a young architect,
was secretary of the Modern Architectural Research Group
which aimed to champion the best in emerging architecture and
design. The Tubbs family came to Wimbledon after their third
child was born. Mary and Ralph, it has been suggested, became
too tired of wheeling prams across the busy road from
Kensington Gore to Kensington Gardens. So apparently Ralph
took out a map and looked for the biggest open space he could
find and Wimbledon caught his eye. The Festival of Britain gave
opportunities to young professionals like Tubbs. The Dome of
Discovery, his contribution to the Festival, was spectacular,
having a diameter twice that of the Albert Hall. There are
obviously similarities here to the Millennium Dome at
Greenwich. Tubbs' other works included Baden Powell House in
South Kensington, the Granada Television Centre in Manchester
and the Charing Cross Hospital at Hammersmith. He also gave a
generous portion of his time and talents to St John's church in
Wimbledon being both Churchwarden and Honorary Treasurer.

1952–1964

Merton Civil Defence display at Merton Public Hall on Kingston Road (see p. 16), 15 September 1955. The gentlemen undertaking the exercise to plot the aftermath of an A-bomb raid are, left to right, Mr Hodgson, Assistant Civil Defence Officer, Mr Warner, Assistant Training Officer, Mr Pearson, Assistant Civil Defence Officer and Mr Holloway, County Training Officer.

Sutton United v. Mitcham and Tooting, *c.* 1955. Football was to become more popular during the 1960s, largely as a result of televised games. Local teams had a proud reputation during this period – Wimbledon Football Club won the FA Amateur Cup in 1963, while Tooting and Mitcham United managed a draw against Nottingham Forest in 1959.

Ken Mackintosh and his Orchestra, *c.* 1951. This is the original band line up, photographed at the Wimbledon Palais (see p. 102). The band was resident there from 1950 to 1953. Its members were Alec McGregor, Stan Hibbett, Bill Morris, Gordon Langhorn, Clive Sharrock, Gerry Gerke, Ronnie Macauley, Ronnie Keane, Jimmy Brown, Bobby Kevin, Jack Seymour, Tommy Watt. The singer was Kenny Bardell. The Palais had visiting bands every Tuesday evening and bandleaders such as Ted Heath, Joe Loss, Jack Parnell and Johnny Dankworth appeared. In addition, The Beatles made an early visit but only for their fan club – those who were there say that the management put barriers around the stage to stop people getting too close to the Fab Four. In 1950 the Palais was taken on by a new management team of Oscar Rabin, Harry Davis and Alec Taylor who ensured the success of the venue for the rest of the decade.

Gun site huts in Carshalton Road used by homeless families as living accommodation, 25 January 1954. A number of anti-aircraft guns had been located on Mitcham Common during the Second World War, including the 3.7-inch guns manned by the Honourable Artillery Company just south of Mitcham Junction station.

Flats at the top of Wimbledon Hill Road, c. 1955. Hill Court was built in the late 1930s. Off to the left are the beginnings of Belvedere Drive. Just beyond the lampposts is the road called Draxmont while to the right, but not in this picture is a similar block to Hill Court, Emerson Court. Note the cyclist, who has evidently decided against riding up the hill, and the luxuriant trees, soon to be ruined by Dutch Elm disease.

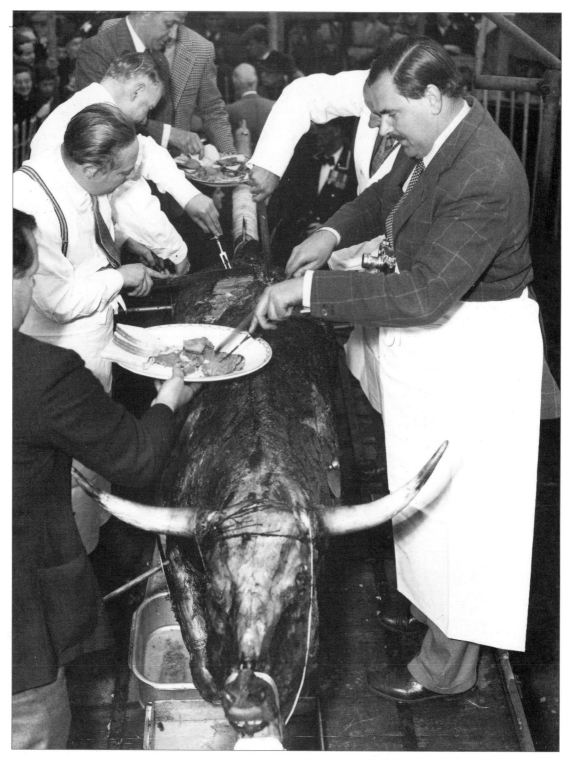

Wimbledon's ox-roast for the coronation, 2 June 1953. Wimbledon's already established tradition of hosting ox-roasts (see p. 11) was continued with this event on Wimbledon Common. The Mayor, Councillor Sydney Black, had left Wimbledon at 6.30 a.m. in order to see the procession for the coronation of Elizabeth II in London, but he was back in the evening to join the hundreds of people around the enclosure at Rushmere where he declared, 'I have never had a joint like this before.'

Coronation flower beds at Tamworth Recreation Ground, 1953. The *Mitcham Gazette* of 13 May 1953, commented: 'What was undoubtedly the best organised procession held in the history of Mitcham was the Chamber of Commerce procession on Saturday in connection with the coronation celebrations. . . . There were entertainments at the stadium, and the programme ended with a grand fireworks display on Three Kings Green.' In Merton and Morden thousands of people converged on Morden Park for the grand finale of coronation night when a torchlight procession approached the park from three different directions. 'God Save the Queen' was shouted and 200 flaming torches ignited the 25ft bonfire.

Mitcham fair, *c.* 1955. There were a number of particularly wet starts to Mitcham fair during the 1950s. Here we see (on a bicycle that looks rather too large for him) a young man attempting to cross Three Kings Piece which had already been scarred, due to the inclement weather, by the heavy trucks and machinery necessary to transport the fair from place to place.

The Majestic cinema, Mitcham, 1962. Mitcham's only cinema closed due to the drop in audiences in 1961. It became a bingo hall, as can be seen here, and casino prior to demolition in the 1970s to make way for a supermarket.

Fishing for tiddlers in Three Kings Pond, 1958. Perhaps one of the most bizarre local news stories of 1999, the year of this book's publication, related to an 'emergency fish rescue' at Three Kings Pond. Over 1,000 fish were removed from the pond in July after concerned residents noticed dead and distressed fish; their problems were blamed on hot weather which lowered water levels and deoxygenated the water. The Environment Agency removed the fish, and four terrapins, leaving perhaps about 100 fish in the pond.

Rushmere Pond, Wimbledon Common, *c.* 1955. This large pond, which was known as Rushmere in Tudor times (when it was a source of rushes widely used in building early huts and cottages), has always been popular with young people for paddling, pond dipping and sailing boats. In the 1930s it froze sufficiently hard to allow ice skating. In the background are the houses on what was once Wimbledon Green.

Members of the Stepping Out Company at the Girls' Training Corps concert, Merton Public Hall, 29 October 1954. This is an excellent example of the large number of pictures surviving from, perhaps, the heyday of the local press. Certainly in the 1950s the local newspapers had their own staff photographers and this resulted in a number of fine 1950s social history collections amassing in many archives and libraries. This image is from the Croydon News group which in the 1950s published the *Morden News*.

Morden Postmen's District Office in Central Road, August 1953. The photograph shows the Assistant Inspector, Mr Jones (centre front), the two Postmen Higher Grade (in brown coats at each end of the back row), the postmen and the cleaner (in beret, second row). Morden Postmen's District Office was opened on Monday 12 March 1934 to serve the new Morden Postal District, mail having previously come through Mitcham. Morden PDO was to come under the control of the Sutton Postal District area, which included Carshalton, Wallington and Banstead. In February 1955 Morden PDO moved to larger premises in London Road. Divided into seven sections Sutton postal district area was postcoded SM. Morden postal district was coded SM4. Taken at the behest of the Assistant Inspector, the photograph includes all the staff except two – the photographer, Mr W.J. Rudd, who kindly loaned the picture for inclusion in this publication, and another postman who refused to join in. Note they are still wearing the original numbered cap badge which had been replaced with a new one with crossed post-horns and a numbered lapel badge after the accession of Queen Elizabeth II the previous year.

Mitcham Cricket XI, 1960/1. The team gave some fine performances against a variety of local, county and international opponents during the 1960s, including a party of visiting South Africans. The players and officials pictured here are left to right, back row: Jim Dawes (Umpire); Vic Hucknall; Jimmy James; Aston Sherwood; Derek Catlin; Cliff Leonard and Ray Catlin. Front row:Clive Peacock; Dennis Catlin; Pat Batty (Captain); Brian Wood and Eaton Swaby.

'Morden car queue', 10 June 1955. A stretch of cars parked *en route* to Morden station by businessmen travelling to London. The original comments from the *Merton & Morden News* included 'an everyday sight near Morden Tube Station are cars which are parked in the area'. However, we are told that the position was particularly bad when this photo was taken due to a rail strike which made it more than usually difficult to reach the city.

Mitcham and District Lambretta Club (the Goons), 1962. The Goons were founded on the growing wave of enthusiasm for bikes and scooters, especially the Italian-designed Vespas and Lambrettas. Second from the right is Mr Duce, who upon attending the 'Mods, Minis and Mayhem' exhibition at Merton Heritage Centre, February–April 1999, duly identified himself in this photo.

Aneurin Bevan speaking at Merton Public Hall, 11 May 1955. Bevan, architect of postwar social reform, attended a meeting in Merton to support the Labour Party's general election campaign. In particular he was supporting the local candidate, Mr Bob Edwards, editor of the Bevanite paper *Tribune*. Bevan said: 'I am delighted to say a word on behalf of one of our really bright young men in the Labour Party. He is charming, intelligent and sincere – all the qualities which make a good candidate and an excellent MP. Since I have known him I have not only developed an admiration for him but a strong affection also.' Bevan's endorsement certainly seemed to help Bob Edwards, who won the election held in May.

Presentation of the Benton Shield at 2157 Squadron, Air Training Corps, 1962. The shield is always awarded to the 'Best Cadet' – the one judged to have developed and achieved most over the previous year.

B. Nichols newsagent, tobacconist, confectioner and stationer, 1954. These premises were at nos 121 and 123 Merton High Street. British people read a huge variety of papers during the 1950s – a regular 600 readers per 1,000 head of population. Note that a number of magazines targeted at women readers and the young are also advertised. Originally these buildings were houses with front gardens but the latter were lost at the beginning of the twentieth century. The premises were demolished during the redevelopment of the area.

Wimbledon Village, c. 1966. The building covered with scaffolding was the original Wimbledon Fire Station. The Wimbledon Society (or as it was then the John Evelyn Society, founded in 1903) organised a 'face lift' scheme for Wimbledon Village and the architects for the work were Alan and Sylvia Blanc. The project, of which the fire station building was a part, was very well received and won a Civic Trust award in 1968.

Flower show at Colliers Wood, 18 August 1956. Despite very poor summer weather, including storms, torrential rain and high winds which were expected to daunt even the most enthusiastic gardener, the 1956 Merton Abbey Horticultural Society summer show at Sunshine Hall attracted a record number of entries, some 400 in total. Councillor W.H. Page, the society's President presented the prizes.

Wimbledon Hill Road, 1950s. On the right, by the bus, is the Alexandra public house. Wimbledon public library is obscured by the large tree in the centre of the picture. The Barclays Bank on the corner of Wimbledon Hill Road and Compton Road is now a part of the All Bar One chain of restaurant bars. Note the trolleybus wires (still there although the actual buses had been replaced), the relaxed cyclists on the right and the small bus coming down Wimbledon Hill Road.

The western part of the High Street, Wimbledon Village, *c.* 1964. The entrance to Eagle House is behind the large tree on the right and the war memorial is in the background.

Rock Terrace, Mitcham, looking towards the site of New Close housing estate and Phipps Bridge Road, 1959. This picture was taken just before the clearance for the new estate began. There were a number of stories in the local press around this time relating to the terrible state of the area. The *Mitcham News & Mercury* printed on 9 January 1959: 'Rock Terrace Recreation Ground – the notorious happy hunting ground for scrap metal merchants – is at last to be cleared. Residents have long complained about what they describe as "the biggest eyesore in the borough". Despite the agreement by the Council to go ahead with a clean up (costed at £7,000) by 21st August still nothing has happened. Mitcham Conservatives are still loudly voicing their disapproval of conditions at Rock Terrace Recreation Ground and nearby Queens and Bath Roads.'

Workers at James Pascall and Company, manufacturers of sugar confectionary, *c.* 1958. A fire at Pascall's Blackfriars works in 1897 forced the firm to find to a new site. The new premises on Streatham Road came to dominate the area until an amalgamation in 1959. Within just a few years the factory was shut down and awaiting demolition. The site has been redeveloped as an industrial estate.

Mitcham Guides Empire Day service, *c.* 1956. Empire Day was first celebrated in 1902 on 24 May, Queen Victoria's birthday, to encourage schoolchildren to be aware of their duties and responsibilities as citizens of the British Empire. Over the years both the name and the date have changed. It is now known as Commonwealth Day and is celebrated on the second Monday in March.

Merton and Morden Urban District Council Public Health Department and Library, 116–18 Kingston Road, *c.* 1958. These offices were built by Merton Parish Council in 1903 and taken over by the new Merton and Morden Urban District Council in 1913. When most council administration moved to Morden Hall in 1942, the building was adopted as a library.

The eastern part of the High Street, Wimbledon, at the junction of Wimbledon Hill, The Ridgway and the High Street, *c.* 1964. To the right of the Westminster Bank building is the site of the Toynbee Fountain (see p. 13). Some of the shops on the left still survive from the 1870s, including the baker's behind the lamppost in the picture. The bank was built after the Belvedere estate was developed in about 1900.

There is known to have been a Crown Inn in Morden since at least 1801. The Crown shown here dates from 1932. Built in a mock Tudor style it offered a number of bars, a function room (the King's Hall), off-licence and children's room. Note, on the left, a flower-seller, a Bedford van, and on the extreme left, Dr Who's Tardis, alias a police call-box, and a wartime relic, an air-raid siren (on top of the pole, next to the police box). This site is now occupied by the Civic Centre and, specifically, the library extension of 1990.

An architect's drawing of Crown House, c. 1960. This huge development by Bernard Sunley and Sons in the centre of Morden was completed in 1961. It has fourteen floors of commercial office space. As part of the development a new Crown pub with street-level bars and an upstairs function room was built on the old village hall site. The old Crown was then demolished and replaced first by a Caters then a Prestos supermarket and finally the new library. Until recently the new Crown was known as Big Hand Mo's, but now its original name has been restored.

1965–1979

Merton Town Hall, *c*. 1970. This was Wimbledon's second Town Hall on this site and was designed by P.J. Hope. It cost £200,000 and was opened by Prince George, later Duke of Kent, in 1931. In 1965 it became the Town Hall for the London Borough of Merton and remained so until the early 1980s when the borough acquired Crown House in Morden for adaptation as a Civic Centre (see p. 88). The Town Hall was criticised by the architectural historian, Nikolaus Pevsner as 'stone faced, symmetrical and dull' but it has been suggested that it looked more like a genuine civic centre than its successor. In May 1988 it was the focus for the large crowds that welcomed the return from Wembley of Wimbledon Football Club with the FA Cup (see p. 107). It is now part of the Centre Court shopping centre.

The last meeting of the Merton and Morden Urban District Council in Morden Hall, March 1965.

Members of the Mitcham Borough Council seated behind the impressive floral display at Tamworth Recreation Ground. Ambitious plans for the Merton and Morden Urban District Council to have a purpose-built civic centre in Morden Park were never realised. The last Mayors of Mitcham and Wimbledon were Alderman W. Lancaster and Alderman George Waller respectively. Merton and Morden, as an Urban District Council, did not have a Mayor but a Chairman, Councillor Vincent Talbot.

'Death of an elm tree'. This is the original caption reproduced from the *Mitcham News* of 14 September 1973: 'Slaughtered not by the Merton Parks Department but by Dutch Elm disease. Last week workmen did the only thing left to do to the Cricket Green elm trees, Mitcham. They chopped them down. Their battle to save them with inoculation fluid had failed.' Note in the background the Tate almshouses, which date back to 1828 and are now Grade II listed buildings.

Demolition of the Carter's Tested Seeds headquarters at Raynes Park, *c.* 1965. The glowing patchwork of fields was replaced by a housing estate, and all that remains of the site are a few flowery names such as Bodnant Gardens, Polesden Gardens and Petworth Gardens. A block in the centre of the estate is called Carter House.

Polished chrome and brass bells on the forecourt of Mitcham Fire Station, 1967. The fire station, set in its little oasis of green along with Vestry Hall and the Cricketers pub, still reminds the passer-by of Mitcham as it used to be. This photograph was taken by R.A. Clerk of Mitcham Camera Club.

Fire at St Mark's church, Wimbledon, 1966. After the devastating blaze the church was completely rebuilt in a contemporary style, and the foundation stone was laid, not by the vicar or the chairman of the Parochial Church Council, but by members of 'many Church traditions but of one faith'.

Postcard view from the Somerset Road end at Wimbledon tennis finals, postmarked 1973. The message on the reverse reads 'My sister and I have been to Wimbledon this week and have seen the lovely tennis – I hope you are bit better – I shall be back for the Fete Hope it will be a lovely day.' Rain on the second Friday resulted in the men's and ladies' singles finals being contested on the Saturday, with play extended to the Sunday to conclude the mixed doubles' semi-final and final.

'Roll up, roll up, all the fun of the fair', April 1968. Although the annual Mitcham fair, held in August, is long established, its success depends on its ability to change with the times. Modern, high-speed rides have gradually superseded the sedate steam carousels. This view, taken near the Jolly Gardeners, is by W.L. Hutchings and is another example of the work of the Mitcham Camera Club.

The London Borough of Merton's first mobile library, 1969. Mr George Whittlesea, the first driver of the mobile, is seen getting into the vehicle with the librarian. When this picture was taken an HGV licence was required to drive the mobile. This is not the case today, for newer models can be driven by anyone with an ordinary licence.

Morden Library, Morden Road, c. 1973. Because of its growing population, Merton and Morden badly needed a new central library (previously the urban district had had to make do with a number of small branch libraries such as that pictured on p. 67) and in 1960 this building was constructed by Surrey County Council. (As an urban district council the Merton and Morden authority was unable to carry out this project itself.) Only thirty years later this building, which also housed a clinic, was unsuitable for modern needs and in 1990 the library relocated to new premises in Crown House, now Merton Civic Centre (see p. 88). The vacant half of the building, on the left-hand side of this picture, is now a doctor's surgery and a chemist's shop.

John L. Coombes, Mayor of Merton, 1971/2. Here Mr Coombes is seen at what appears to be a prize giving event in Morden Park. The borough elections of 1972 led to the Labour Party gaining control of the council for the first time since the London Borough of Merton was formed in 1965. It was an eventful year for Mr Coombes. Not only did he have a hectic schedule of civic duties to perform, but also shortly before being made Mayor he broke his leg. Later that year, on a rather happier note, he celebrated his golden wedding anniversary.

Merton Abbey First School, High Path, *c.* 1970. Accommodation at the old Abbey Road Infants' School was barely adequate by the beginning of the twentieth century. For many years the local council pushed the county council to provide a replacement. The First World War was one of many causes of delay and it was not until 1927 that a new school opened in this attractive building in High Path. Through changing educational theories and school systems it has laid the foundation of many children's education in its various roles as a junior mixed and infants, primary, and first school.

A domestic science class at William Morris Middle School, 1975. The original building – a single-storey, open-plan design – was opened in early 1973, but 80 per cent of it was destroyed by fire in the early hours of Saturday 20 March 1993. It was rebuilt. The school was named after the socialist, artist and designer William Morris who in 1881 established his works at Merton Abbey (see p. 23).

Merton's Mayor, Alderman Peter Kenyon, lending a hand with preparations for the festivities marking Wimbledon Village's jubilee celebrations, June 1977. In addition to other festivities in Wimbledon for the jubilee, in July a young crowd waited to greet the Queen at the top of Wimbledon Hill as she made her way towards the ladies' singles final at the Centenary Championships. The final was won by the English player Virginia Wade.

Silver Jubilee, 1977. Street parties were held throughout the country to celebrate the twenty-five years of Queen Elizabeth II's reign. Here a festive feast is in full swing in Dalton Avenue, Mitcham. Other photographs within the Local Studies collection show activities such as an orange-and-spoon race, numerous other street and fancy dress parties and a whole host of activities to celebrate the day.

South Wimbledon (Merton) station in the mid-1970s. The station's name has always been the subject of debate because the street on which it stands is called Merton High Street (one side of which is in Wimbledon) and the station itself is in Merton. However, despite a number of requests to reconsider the name, there has never been a firm proposal to alter the existing nomenclature. This junction, now universally known as South Wimbledon after the station, used to be referred to as The Grove, after the fine house – Merton Grove – which used to stand on the opposite corner.

A train approaching the level-crossing in Kingston Road, 1977. This view has since changed. The line now carries the tram service between Wimbledon and Croydon (see p. 123). The gates shown here are from a previous transport generation and the Bottle & Basket off-licence is now Finch's Estate Agency.

Pollards Hill library, *c*. 1973. Opened in 1970 to replace the earlier (1948) building (see p. 67), this showpiece library was part of the award-winning design by P.J. Whittle for a low-rise, high-density housing estate which replaced earlier pre-fabs.

'Serenity', *c*. 1975. This view of the Watermeads estate in Mitcham, was taken from Ravensbury Park. The construction of the estate was partly inspired by the successful Pollards Hill development, although technical problems meant that the scheme had to be scaled down considerably. The park was once part of the estate of the Bidder family.

Morden Park Pool, *c.* 1968. Ever since the formation of Merton and Morden Urban District in 1913, there had been pressure to provide a swimming-pool. Plans were interrupted by the First World War, by the hard times that followed and again in 1939 by the outbreak of the Second World War. The completion of the pool project eventually became an early success for the new London Borough of Merton. It was opened in 1967 by Lord Hunt, who led the successful Everest expedition of 1953. In addition to its modern diving pit, 12ft 6in deep, it had the advantage of a beautiful setting in the grounds of Morden Park House. The pool was not destined to stand alone for long; even before it was opened, permission had been granted to move the Technical College to a new site in the park.

Wimbledon Palais, perhaps more accurately Furnitureland, Merton High Street, *c.* 1979. The Palais has had a colourful history; it was built as a skating rink, used an airship and balloon factory, a dance hall (the Ted Heath Band played there in the 1950s and The Beatles in the 1960s), and most recently as a Furnitureland store. A further chapter in its history is about to be written as there are plans to redevelop the site. The Palais was been a much loved venue, especially in the 1950s when Ken Mackintosh's big band played there (see p. 72).

Sir Cyril and Lady Black, *c.* 1966. Sir Cyril Black was at various times Justice of the Peace, a councillor, Mayor and a Member of Parliament for Wimbledon. A great champion of Wimbledon Borough, he, with many others, was bitterly opposed to its being swallowed up in the borough of Merton. Here he is seen with his wife Dorothy.

The centenary celebrations of the passing of the Wimbledon and Putney Commons Act on the common, 1971. The Act secured this important open space for the people. Here we see a cavalcade in period costume.

The opening of Tesco's, Mitcham, 1970s. The supermarket stands on the site of the London House Stores, which was owned by the renowned local photographer Tom Francis and sold hardware, haberdashery and clothing. The Merton Borough Plan of 1979 expressed concern about the small number and limited range of shops in Mitcham, and the St Mark's Road development was probably a result.

Ely's corner in Wimbledon, 1977. The shop has undergone a number of transformations since Joseph Ely first set up his 'Tailor's, Mercer's and Draper's Store' on the corner of Alexandra Road in Wimbledon in 1876. Ten years later he took over a large house at the corner of Worple Road and turned it into a second, much larger shop.

An aerial view of Colliers Wood, 1978. The tower block and its distinctive circular multi-storey car park have for many years been the home of Brown & Root, the oil exploration company. The tower is officially called Brown & Root Tower, but has also been known as Lyon Tower, and longer ago, Apex Tower. In the foreground are Christ Church and the now-demolished Dickinson Robinson packaging factory. Just visible to the right of the tower is Colliers Wood Tube station, and Wandle Park, Connolly's leather works and the Wandle Valley sewage works can be seen in the distance.

The mosque, Wimbledon Park, 1979. Situated at 260–70 Durnsford Road, Wimbledon Park, the mosque was established in 1977. On Fridays the congregation quite often exceeds 550. The mosque also offers Arabic and Quran classes as well as advice and counselling to its worshippers. Soon after the original mosque was built it was enlarged to its present size. It is a reminder of the diversity of Merton's community.

Buddhist Temple, Wimbledon. Although the building was not officially opened until 1982, the construction of the temple began in 1979. Subsequently, the temple has become a much respected landmark in Wimbledon. The lake in the gardens is the remaining northern part of Margin Lake, which was created for Wimbledon House in 1777.

1980–1999

Celebrations in central Wimbledon, opposite Ely's department store (see p. 104) in 1988, after Wimbledon FC upset the odds and a lot of people's expectations by beating Liverpool 1–0 in the FA Cup Final. Sadly the club moved from their Plough Lane ground in 1991 and have yet to return to the borough.

Wimbledon Windmill in the snow, 1991. The windmill is the only surviving hollow post-mill in the south-east of Britain. In 1997 the Wimbledon and Putney Commons Conservators and the Wimbledon Windmill Museum Trust applied to the Heritage Lottery Fund for a grant of £88,500 to undertake a scheme of restoration works. The application was successful and the grant contributed to the £100,000 cost of restoring the sails, shutters and striking gear, internal building works to link the ground and first floors and the enlargement of the museum. The Windmill Museum was officially reopened on 26 May 1999.

The waterwheel at Merton Abbey Mills, c. 1995. 15ft in diameter and 12ft wide, it generated 15 horsepower in the nineteenth century when is was used as part of what became the Liberty print works (see p. 21). The waterwheel is still active and now supplies power for a potter and a wood turner on the Merton Abbey Mills site.

Merton Admirals American Football
Club, 1989. There was an explosion
of interest in American football
across the UK in the late 1980s.
The Merton Admirals played their
games at what was the *News of the
World* ground – a space alongside
the Canons Leisure Centre,
Commonside West, Mitcham. The
eighteenth-century Park Place,
Commonside West, was used
between the wars as the clubhouse
of the *News of the World*
Organisation. This is another
photograph taken by a member of
the Mitcham Camera Club, in this
case Mr K. Barvell of Morden.

Cycling through Mitcham, June
1988. The cyclists were on the way
from Clapham Common to Brighton
on a fund-raising event for the
British Heart Foundation. This is
now an annual occasion and a
good opportunity to raise money for
a very worthwhile venture. Here
the cyclists are passing Mitcham
Junction station (see p. 39) and
Mitcham Common.

Savacentre at Colliers Wood, c. 1995. This huge retail development (designed to reflect the appearance of the Crystal Palace) was built on land which was once occupied by New Merton Board Mills. This major development opened on Tuesday 28 February 1989. The store's 150,000 square feet cover much of the site of Merton Priory, once one of the most important religious houses in the country. The remains of the chapter house are open for conducted tours and are used for dramatic productions. It has been suggested that the site now hosts a 'Cathedral to Consumerism'.

The Tandem Works, Colliers Wood, late 1980s. The factory was built at the end of the nineteenth century for the Tandem Smelting Syndicate. In 1917 it passed into the ownership of the Eyre Smelting Company and became the largest white-metal works in Europe. Later the works were taken over by Fry's Metals and Fry's Diecastings but the Tandem name was retained. Merton Council, wishing to maintain the industrial character of the site, refused a planning application for retail use in the mid-1990s. This was overturned on appeal to the Secretary of State and the heavily contaminated site was cleared. The Tandem Retail Park (which perpetuates the 100-year-old Tandem name) was opened in 1998, and includes stores owned by Boots, Next, Comet and other national retailers. The site is almost adjacent to Savacentre (above).

'Countryside Comes to Town' event, May 1990. This popular event has been held every May Day Bank Holiday in Morden Hall Park since 1987. Here we see a crowd of children watching some of the entertainment provided during the day. Events and displays have, over the years, included conservation exhibitions, farm animals, Punch and Judy, fire eating and food tasting.

Wimbledon Park sailing base, August 1994. Merton may be a long way from the sea but youngsters can learn sailing skills from qualified instructors at the Wimbledon Park Sailing Centre on what was once an ornamental lake constructed by 'Capability' Brown in the 1760s for the first Earl Spencer.

Fire destroys Woolworth's store, the Broadway, Wimbledon, 30 April 1981. One of the worst incidents in recent years, this blaze resulted in injuries to three firefighters and the death of a fourth. Despite all the heroic efforts of the brigade the shop was completely burnt out, but has since been rebuilt.

Air ambulance at Queen Alexandra's Court, St Mary's Road, Wimbledon, 1995. Here we see paramedics airlifting an injured man to hospital by helicopter. The accident in which he was hurt took place in central Wimbledon and the helicopter landed in the grounds of Queen Alexandra's Court in St Mary's Road. The use of helicopters has made a substantial difference to the task of getting emergency casualties to hospital when traffic congestion causes delays to conventional ambulances. However, unsurprisingly, they are costly to run. The residential buildings shown here were built in 1904–5 and now form part of the borough's architectural heritage, being Grade II listed buildings. They were designed by Ernest George and Yeates with C.E.L. Parkinson and are part of the Royal Homes for Widows and Daughters of Naval and Military Officers.

Wimbledon station, after refurbishment, summer 1998. In 1998 the station had a facelift, which included moving the taxi rank back to its original site at the side of the building (see p. 15). A short time after this picture was taken 2 metre laser-cut steel panels (images of shoppers, commuters and visitors to Wimbledon by designer and artist Bruce Williams) were hoisted into place on top of the station building and along the kerb. The station facelift was co-ordinated by Railtrack, Merton Council and Arrowcroft, and was funded by the All England Tennis Club and Government Office for London. Note also the electronic information board on the right (see also p. 126).

A view of modern Morden from the top of Merton Civic Centre, December 1996. Note the underground station and bus terminus on the left and, to the right, the Iceland supermarket where the Morden Cinema once stood (see p. 48).

Greensleeves Morris Men with Mayor Vincent Talbot and his wife, Wimbledon Common May Day, 6.30 a.m 1982. Many old English folk customs have continued into the modern age. Here Morris men have been welcoming the May Day dawn. It is believed that Morris dancing has Moorish origins, but the reasons for its association with May, bells attached to clothing and the hobby horse are not entirely clear.

A picnic at Cannizaro Park, pre-1987. Cannizaro House (see p. 66) and 34 acres of land were sold to the Corporation of Wimbledon by the Countess of Munster in 1948. While the house was eventually sold into private hands and became a hotel in 1987, the park has been open to the public since 1948 and is the venue for an annual summer open-air theatre festival run by Wimbledon Theatre.

Merton's float from the Lord Mayor's Show. In 1988 Sir Christopher Collet, a Wimbledon resident, became the new Lord Mayor of London. To represent the London Borough of Merton, the Wimbledon School of Art designed a float and costumes. Illustrated here are music and art, famous residents, Lord Nelson and Emma Hamilton, with period Wimbledon tennis players and Mitcham lavender girls. Other figures included Mitcham cricketers, Wimbledon footballers and red-headed sailors.

Fiftieth Anniversary of VE (Victory in Europe) Day beacon in Morden Hall Park, 8 May 1995. There was widespread support for the events to mark the fiftieth anniversary of the end of the Second World War in Europe and in addition to the commemoration shown here, a multi-faith service was held on 20 August (VJ or Victory over Japan Day) to commemorate those who served in the conflict. The service of remembrance in Ravensbury Park included the planting of a grove of peace. Deacon Fred Carter of St John Fisher church summarised the thoughts of many: 'In 1995 we should be thankful that for the last fifty years we have been without the dreadful massacre that we experienced in the years 1939 to 1945.'

The late Labour Party leader John Smith visited Merton shortly before his tragic death in May 1994. He visited Hatfeild First School and the Civic Centre. Here he is seen entering the Civic Centre with the then Leader of the Council Anthony Colman (now MP for Putney). The end of the millennium was an historic time for the Labour Party in Merton. In the general election of 1997, Merton elected two Labour MPs for the first time ever, Siobhain McDonagh for Mitcham and Morden and Roger Casale for Wimbledon – the first time the Wimbledon constituency had a Labour MP since the 1945 election.

Morden station, 1998. Designed by Charles Holden, this was the City and South London Railway terminus of the Morden–Edgware line, renamed the Northern Line by London Transport in 1937. By the 1960s a three-storey office block named Station House had been incorporated into the frontage, with a separate entrance in a gap between the shops at the south end. By 1988 this was named Athena House and a second entrance to the north was named Apollo House.

The Mayor of Merton, Councillor Marie-Louise de Villiers, unveils the relocated and refurbished clock tower in Mitcham town centre, Saturday 23 April 1994. The Jubilee Clock was first erected in 1898 to commemorate Queen Victoria's diamond jubilee in 1897. It was originally located on the Fair Green, Mitcham.

Canons House, Mitcham, 1997. The Canons, one of the largest houses in Mitcham, was built in the late seventeenth century. It was one of the properties on the Cranmer estate and was named after the canons of St Mary Overy at Southwark who owned the land until the Dissolution of the monasteries in the sixteenth century. In 1939 the estate was purchased by the Corporation of Mitcham. As late as the 1940s the grounds possessed several fine and exotic trees. The carp pond undoubtedly pre-dates the Dissolution, as does the pigeon house which is probably the oldest complete building in Mitcham. Containing 400 nesting places, it is constructed of brick and chalk blocks, on one of which the date MDXI (1511) is inscribed. The Canons Leisure Centre, built in the grounds, was opened in September 1983. The basement of the house itself was converted into Merton Heritage Centre and was officially opened by the Mayor in April 1994 on the same day but shortly after the event pictured above.

The Polka Theatre, Wimbledon Broadway, summer 1998. The Polka Theatre for Children is the only theatre building in Britain that produces and presents work exclusively for the country's youngest audiences. The main building was originally a large church hall and two shop premises belonging to Holy Trinity church. The theatre acquired these premises in 1977/8, and added to them in 1983. The main theatre seats 300 people and generally stages performances for children aged between five and thirteen. A smaller space is used for productions for younger children.

Children at Deen City Farm, 1998. The farm was founded in Aberdeen Road, Mitcham, in 1978. In 1980 it moved to Batsworth Road where it flourished for fourteen years before the site was developed for housing. In October 1994 it was transferred to its present site in Windsor Avenue, Merton Abbey – a purpose-built farm on land formerly known as Bunce's Meadow, now owned by the National Trust.

The Prince of Wales public house, Wimbledon, summer 1997. The Prince of Wales has been a landmark on the corner of Hartfield Road since at least 1867 when an early proprietor (Mr William Amos Eagles) appeared in the *Metallurgicon* local directory. In 1997 it was refurbished and repainted – the reason for this photograph – and coincidentally at the time of writing it is undergoing another refit.

St George's House, St George's Road, Wimbledon, 1998. The building provides office space for a number of companies and replaced the South-Western Hotel (in 1865 the Mansel Tavern) and Mansel Villas, which were built in 1870. In addition to private parking for its own occupants, it also incorporates an underground car park for the public. Wimbledon has undergone something of a transformation in the last twenty years and there have been a number of controversial developments. (See p. 123, lower picture, for a view of the so-called 'Fridge on the Bridge' known more formally as Wimbledon Bridge House.)

121

A result of the 'Great Storm', 181 Manor Road, Mitcham, 16 October 1987. Merton's Local Studies Centre holds many photographs of the consequences of this meteorological event. The storm established the weatherman, Michael Fish, as a media celebrity. His uncompromising rejection of the possible approach of a hurricane during the BBC weather report the previous evening has been impossible to live down. On the night of 15/16 October a large number of people around Merton and across the country were to find out that the weatherman is not always right.

An unwanted paddling pool in Merton Park, 1992. In addition to tackling flames, firefighters often use high-powered pumping equipment to relieve flooding. The incident pictured here resulted from a burst water main in Mayfield Road. The first main was put down in 1850 and is still in use, but the new London ring main has taken some of the pressure off the old pipework.

South Merton station on the Wimbledon–Sutton line, August 1998. Built by the Southern Railway and opened in 1930, it has now undergone refurbishment by current owners Railtrack (which controls train lines throughout the United Kingdom) and Thameslink, which manages the station. The ambitious renovation scheme on the Thameslink loop extension to Sutton and West Croydon included Wimbledon Chase, South Merton, Morden South and St Helier stations, which were extensively upgraded and redecorated. Old, dark, dank and unpleasant stations were demolished, a new colour scheme was introduced and the whole service was made much more approachable. Problems remain, as ever, around reliability and the frequency of the service in and out of Wimbledon.

A tram on the Croydon Tramlink leaving Wimbledon for Croydon, April 1999. To accompany this photograph a press release was issued by Tramlink Croydon Limited (TCL). The Project Director, Mr Ian Kendall said: 'We are proud to have achieved the critical milestone of getting trams into Wimbledon Station. The whole Project Team is to be commended for their efforts. The next major milestone is to achieve trams on the Central Croydon route in June 1999.' The Croydon Tramlink Scheme is a £200 million Private Finance Initiative project awarded to TCL in November 1996. The Tramlink was tested at all stages of construction by Her Majesty's Railway Inspectorate, a member of which is seen on the left. Mr Kendall added: 'The Wimbledon to Wandle Park leg will now begin to see more intensive tram running as we commence driver training in May [1999]. Finally, on behalf of TCL I would like to thank the residents of the London Borough of Merton for their patience through the difficult construction phase which is now clearly nearing completion.'

Wimbledon's Centre Court shopping centre, April 1994. The redevelopment of the Town Hall (see p. 89) was undertaken in 1990. The rotunda built as part of the redevelopment is clearly seen here; as this book goes to print additional works are being undertaken on the façade of the Town Hall building. The development also retained the frontages of the fire station (see p. 20) and the Baptist Church, in Queen's Road.

A South West Trains service about to depart from platform 8, Wimbledon station, c. 1996. Wimbledon station is a public transport hub for the London Borough of Merton. As well as receiving South West Trains services to southerly destinations and Waterloo, Wimbledon is also the terminus for the District Line Underground service from Edgware Road and for some services from the City. In addition, it is on the route of the Thameslink services from Luton and Bedford to Sutton. Croydon Tramlink uses part of platform 10, and this means that platform 9 is difficult to operate for Thameslink trains coming from both directions. Plans exist to connect the other part of platform 10 to the East London Line of the Underground. The ever-increasing need to reduce traffic congestion and encourage journeys by public transport will ensure Wimbledon station's future as a central part of Merton's transport infrastructure.

Children of the Millennium Woodland, 1999. School children from St John Fisher Roman Catholic First School with some of the hundreds of acorns that were planted in preparation for the Merton Millennium Woodland project. This joint initiative between the Education, Leisure and Libraries Department, Trees for London and the schools of Merton will result in the creation of an oakwood on St Joseph Hood Memorial Playing Fields, New Malden. Schoolchildren, students, staff from Merton Civic Centre and members of the general public all had an opportunity to plant acorns supplied by Merton's arboricultural officers. Members of the Millennium Team gave talks about trees, the environment and the project to all classes involved and to school assemblies. Visits to the area continued throughout 1999 to ensure that the young oaks were protected and watered. Planting out of the tiny trees was due to start at the end of 1999 and continue for several weeks.

Siobhain McDonagh MP, signing a book of condolence after the tragic deaths of Diana, Princess of Wales, and Dodi Fayed in August 1997. The outpouring of grief after the terrible accident in Paris was unprecedented in Britain. The people of Merton joined millions across the world in expressing their grief at the loss of the 'People's Princess'. Streams of people waited patiently to sign the books of condolence or simply to lay flowers in respect. Diana, as a tennis fan, was a regular visitor to the royal box for the All England Championships and to Wimbledon restaurants.

Merton's future. The council's first electronic noticeboard and children from St Mary's Roman Catholic Primary School, Wimbledon, June 1998. It seems appropriate to reproduce the original caption as it appeared in the *Merton Messenger*: 'We've gone dotty about public information! Merton has its first electronic information board outside Wimbledon Station. And, as pupils Nathan Richards (8), Suzanna Unsworth (9), Lucy Abisogun (9) and Jo Newham (8) from St Mary's RC School in Wimbledon discovered, there is a great range of Council and community information to be read.'

Acknowledgements

To all the members of staff who have helped me I would like to say a thank you: Susan Andrew, Heather Constance, Rosemary Doyle, Edwina Farlow, Sarah Gould, Adrian Hare, Jean Henderson, Annemarie Riding, Wendy Siemaszko. A particular mention of Gordon Brewin and Pam Rew for continual reminders of approaching deadlines also seems appropriate.

Although it is important to acknowledge the many donations to the Local Studies Centre and Heritage Centre, both documented and anonymous, that have helped enable me to produce this work, I would also like to thank the Croydon News Group, Environmental Services Department, John Innes Society, Merton Heritage Centre, Merton Press Office, Mitcham Camera Club, Polka Theatre, Tramlink Croydon and the Wimbledon Society for allowing me to use a small selection from their photographic collection in this book. The few reproduced are a small selection and there are many others that are worthy of inclusion in a book of this type. Also, thanks to the many individuals who have supplied or agreed to allow me to use their photographs, in particular Ken Mackintosh, Bill Rudd and Margaret Stocker. I should also like to acknowledge a personal debt to the many other organisations and individuals, both within Merton Council and beyond, who have helped with this venture, especially colleagues past and present within the Library and Heritage Services and also the wider Education, Leisure and Libraries Department for their contributions or advice towards this publication.

Mention must also be made of those individuals who have proofed the typescript: Frank Coffey, Rosemary Doyle, Cyril Maidment, Richard Milward, Eric Montague, Norman Plastow and Bill Rudd. Many thanks for your endeavours and for ironing out the inevitable mistakes. As ever, any remaining errors are my responsibility.

Finally, my family have showed patience and some degree of interest; thanks and lots of love to Lorraine, Laura and James. And Paul – you know who you are.

Bibliography

Goodman, Judith, *Merton and Morden: A Pictorial History* (1995)
Harris, Nick, *Mitcham* (1996)
Loobey, Patrick, *Merton, Morden and Mitcham* (1996)
Merton & Morden News
Milward, Richard, *Wimbledon: A Pictorial History* (1994)
——, *Wimbledon 1865–1965* (1997)
——, *Wimbledon Past* (1998)
Mitcham News & Mercury
Montague, Eric, *Mitcham: A Pictorial History* (1991)
——, (ed.), *Old Mitcham* (1993)
Wimbledon Borough News

Index